ACCOUNTING & COMMUNICATION

Maurice L. Hirsch, Jr.
Southern Illinois University at Edwardsville

Rob Anderson
St. Louis University

Susan Gabriel
Southern Illinois University at Edwardsville

COLLEGE DIVISION   South-Western Publishing Co.
Cincinnati Ohio

Editor-in-Chief: Mark R. Hubble
Acquisitions Editor: David L. Shaut
Developmental Editor: Ann Sass
Production Editors: Thomas E. Shaffer, Eric Carlson
Production House: WordCrafters Editorial Services, Inc.
Cover Designer: Lotus Wittkopf
Marketing Manager: Michael O'Brien

AB80AA
Copyright © 1994
By South-Western Publishing Co.
Cincinnati, Ohio

ALL RIGHTS RESERVED
The text of this publication, or any part thereof, may not be reproduced or transmitted in any form or by any means, electronic or mechanical, including photocopying, recording, storage in an information retrieval system, or otherwise, without the prior written permission of the publisher.

Library of Congress Cataloging-in-Publication Data

Hirsch, Maurice L.
    Accounting & communication / Maurice L. Hirsch, Jr., Rob Anderson, Susan Gabriel.
      p. cm.
    Includes bibliographical references.
    ISBN 0-538-83177-4
    1. Business communication. 2. Accounting. I. Anderson, Rob.
II. Gabriel, Susan L. (Susan Laine). III. Title.
IV. Title: Accounting and communication.
HF5718.H575   1993
657—dc20   93-39271
                                                                                                      CIP

1 2 3 4 5 6 7 MA 9 8 7 6 5 4 3
Printed in the United States of America

I(T)P
International Thomson Publishing

South-Western Publishing Co. is an ITP Company. The ITP trademark is used under license.

About the Authors

The writing team reflects the basic integrative purpose of the book.

Maurice L. Hirsch, Jr., Professor of Accounting, Southern Illinois University at Edwardsville, is the co-author with Joseph G. Louderback III of *Cost Accounting: Accumulation, Analysis, and Use*, Third Edition (South-Western, 1992), and author of *Advanced Management Accounting*, Second Edition (South-Western, 1994).

Rob Anderson, Professor of Communication, Saint Louis University, has worked with the other two co-authors in developing a workshop sequence in communication for accounting students. Anderson is the author or co-author of *Students as Real People: Interpersonal Communication and Education* (Hayden, 1979), *Before the Story: Interviewing and Communication Skills for Journalists* (St. Martin's Press, 1989), and *Questions of Communication: A Practical Introduction to Theory* (St. Martin's Press, 1994).

Susan L. Gabriel, Director, Corporate Writing Program, Southern Illinois University at Edwardsville, was part of an ongoing program to involve readers from the English Department in assessing the work of accounting students. She is the guiding force and prime facilitator for the workshop, "Writing Across the Business Curriculum," required for all School of Business faculty at Southern Illinois University at Edwardsville. She has joined Hirsch in regional and national presentations on accounting and communication as well as collaborating on a *Journal of Accounting Education* article in this area. Gabriel provides workshops and seminars for area businesses to improve corporate communication. She is the co-editor of *Gender in the Classroom: Power and Pedagogy* (University of Illinois Press, 1990).

Preface

> Accounting is an artifact—a product of human intervention designed by humans for human purposes.[1]

Purpose

Accounting and Communication focuses on the human dimensions of accounting: communication and interaction. Developing effective communication skills both in writing and speaking is essential for every accounting professional. Successful communication is achieved through careful thinking and planning; this book offers strategies for thinking through and developing a communication plan for a variety of communication contexts in the accounting field.

Accounting is primarily concerned with the accumulation, analysis, communication, and use of information. By its very nature, accounting (and the role accountants play) requires that its practitioners have excellent writing, speaking, reading, listening, and questioning skills. In the past, however, there has been an artificial division in how communication skills have been taught. Writing has been separated from speaking, and technical matters have been so separated from communication skills that eliciting information and listening skills have been generally ignored. In addition, insufficient attention has been paid to the clear link between communication and thinking skills. This book creates no such artificial divisions and seeks to help readers solve these problems.

As professionals, we value all forms of communication that might be encountered by those in accounting-related positions as well by managers in general. These forms include information presentation and reception both in oral and written formats, in one-to-one, one-to-many, and group discussion contexts. In addition, we believe thinking and communication are inseparable. Thus, our approach in this book is to address the convergence of the writing/speaking and thinking processes.

All communication involves a series of choices; making choices involves critical thinking. This concept is a way of focusing on the creative control each person exercises over his or her messages. However, the writer or speaker has to make choices in communication that are dependent on a string of variables, including purpose, audience, role,

---

[1] L. Parker, K. Ferris, and D. Otley, *Accounting for the Human Factor* (Sydney: Prentice-Hall of Australia Pty. Ltd., 1989), p. 1.

and context. Individuals can develop thinking strategies to aid in this creative process and to make the entire process of communication less threatening and intimidating.

Intended Audience

We've written this book primarily for students majoring in accounting, for whom it can serve as reference and guide from the sophomore year through graduate school. Two other audiences will benefit: other undergraduate business majors as well as practicing accountants (public, private, governmental) and managers. The book is a helpful supplement to all accounting courses and a useful reference guide for the practitioner's professional library.

What's Included and What's Not

The primary audience is students at the sophomore level and above who have completed their general course requirements in English and Speech Communication. In addition, we assume students will use this book in conjunction with such professional resources as a dictionary, a thesaurus, and a writing/style manual; therefore, we concentrate on the larger communication issues that affect accountants, with emphasis on the main problem areas of grammar and usage. These larger communication issues include the following essential topics:

- understanding the relationship of thinking and communication
- determining purpose
- analyzing an audience
- organizing a presentation
- preparing a draft
- editing a text
- working with a word processor
- dealing with stage fright
- overcoming writer's block
- speaking and writing with confidence
- interviewing
- listening
- communicating in formal and informal contexts
- coordinating group projects
- developing visual aids
- understanding nonverbal communication

Because readers will have varying skill levels, backgrounds, and experience, we have developed a wide range of examples and exercises. Obviously, not all examples or exercises will be equally accessible to every reader, but professionals and students alike should find explanations to be basic and practical.

General Structure

Our goal is to integrate material on writing and speaking skills rather than to have a single, separate chapter or section devoted to oral communication: face-to-face talk has been seriously undervalued in professional skills training. As appropriate, each chapter deals with common issues followed by how these same concerns can be specially addressed in speaking or writing situations.

Each chapter includes *Situations*, examples of problems from both the business and academic worlds. These examples encourage the reader to think through the chapter concepts within practical settings. Instructors can assign specific *Situations* to be completed by their students; however, individual readers can benefit by considering their responses to the various contexts presented in the *Situations*. Suggested solutions for selected *Situations* are included at the end of each chapter. In addition, the Instructor's Manual includes suggestions relating to all *Situations*.

Since this is a supplemental book to be used in financial, management, auditing, systems, and tax accounting classes, instructors are encouraged to choose texts and cases that incorporate specific written and oral assignments as well as to redesign existing text problems and cases. The Instructor's Manual expands on this point.

This book is written in a style that engages the reader directly with practical, viable strategies and suggestions that can be applied both to course work and on-the-job tasks. Since this is a handbook, the reader can browse through it to find needed information. While there are some chapters that a reader will study from beginning to end, others will allow the reader to select only those parts that fit his or her needs. Besides a regular Table of Contents, we also include a Topical Table of Contents to aid in this process.

Instructor's Manual

The Instructor's Manual is a comprehensive guide to incorporating thinking and communication skills within accounting courses. Much in the way that the book is an ongoing reference to its readers, the Instructor's Manual provides a resource to those who teach accounting. Instructors will learn how to choose different types of assignments, how to design assignments, how to give feedback, what to consider when grading, how to develop and utilize partnerships with English and Speech Communication faculty, what resources (technical, financial, human) are available, how the scope of overall course content is affected by integrating communication skills in a course, and how examinations and grade weights are affected.[2]

Acknowledgments

We wish to thank the following reviewers for their helpful evaluation, criticism, and suggestions during the development of this book.

Michael Costigan, *Southern Illinois University at Edwardsville*

Lynn Griffen, *North Carolina Agricultural Tech*

George Heyman, *Oakton Community College*

Debra Kerby, *Northeast Missouri State University*

Linda Lovata, *Southern Illinois Univeristy at Edwardsville*

Patti Mills, *Indiana State University*

Andrew Rosman, *University of Connecticut*

Fred Sellers, *Southwestern University*

Ronald Tidd, *Syracuse University*

Stanley Tonge, *University of Minnesota*

Loren Wenzel, *Mankato State University*

---

[2] Much of the basic philosophy of the Instructor's Manual comes from S. Gabriel and M. Hirsch, "Critical Thinking and Communication Skills: Integration and Implementation Issues." *Journal of Accounting Education* 10,2 (Fall 1992): 243–270.

Contents

About the Authors — iii
Preface — v
Topical Table of Contents — xv

INTRODUCTION
ACCOUNTING AND COMMUNICATION — 1

1 Communicating in Accounting — 3
  Communication: The Core of Accounting 4
    Role of Accountants 4
    Ways We Can Communicate 4
  Types of Communication 5
  Critical Thinking and Communication:
      An Inseparable Combination 6
  Situation 1: Assessing an Assignment 7
  Strategies for Clear Thinking 7
  Situation 2: Thinking Through a Task 8
  Necessary Communication Skills 8
    Basic Skills Assumed 11
    You Must Be an Active Learner 11
    What's Included in This Book 11
  Summary 11
  How to Approach Selected Situations — 13
  Appendix: Suggested Background Material — 15
    Writing and Reading 15
    Speaking and Listening 15

PART ONE
DEVELOPING A COMMUNICATION PLAN — 17

2 Analyzing Context and Purpose — 19
  Communication: Beyond Transmission 20
    The Traditional Model 20
    Interactive Communication 21

Developing a Communication Plan   23
Communicator Roles   25
   Accountants' Roles   25
   Roles in Organizational Context   26
Situation 1: Writing Memos Based on Roles   28
Differences Between Written and Oral Communication   29
   Practical Considerations   29
Strategies for Written Communication   30
Strategies for Oral Communication   31
Situation 2: Shaping a Message Based on Role and Audience   33
Summary   34
How to Approach a Selected Situation   35

3 Analyzing the Audience   37

The Role of Audience   37
Situation 1: Writing a Memo for Different Audiences   38
Writer-Centered Versus Reader-Centered Texts   38
Situation 2: Rewriting Writer-Centered Texts   39
The Process of Audience Analysis   39
   Who Will Be Receiving This Message?   39
   What Is My Relationship to This Audience?   41
   What Does My Audience Already Know
      About This Subject?   41
Situation 3: Creating Messages for Different Audiences   42
   What Does My Audience Need to Know
      About This Subject?   43
   What Are My Audience's Feelings
      About This Subject?   43
*Situation 4: Shaping Communication
   for Specific Audiences*   44
   What Cultural Differences Might Influence
      How My Audience Will Read or Hear Messages?   44
Audience Analysis Strategies for
   Written Communication   45
Audience Analysis Strategies for
   Oral Communication   46
*Situation 5: Developing Oral Presentations
   for Specific Audiences*   48
Summary   49
How to Approach a Selected Situation   51

4 Determining Content and Approach — 53
Content as Part of a Communication Plan   53
Deciding on an Approach   54
   Analysis Versus Description   54
   Formal Versus Informal Approach   55
Situation 1: Recognizing Analysis and Description   56
Situation 2: Choosing Between Formal and Informal Approaches   57
   Direct Versus Indirect Approach   57
Situation 3: Creating an Indirect and a Direct Text   58
Choosing an Organizational Scheme   59
   The Three S's   59
   Topical Organization   60
   Chronological Order   60
   Cause-Effect or Effect-Cause   61
   Decreasing Order of Importance   61
   Increasing Order of Importance   61
Summary and Synthesis   62
   Preparing a Summary   62
Situation 4: Summarizing   63
   Synthesis   63
Situation 5: Synthesizing Information   65
Sources of Information   65
Deciding on Graphics   66
   Tables   67
   Figures   68
   Computer Graphics   70
Summary   72
How to Approach Selected Situations   73

PART TWO
IMPLEMENTING A COMMUNICATION PLAN — 75

5 Creating a Text — 77
From Plan to Text   77
Turning Blank Pages into Drafts   79
   Drafting as Experimenting   79
   Inventing a Draft: Getting Started   79
Situation 1: Brainstorming and Clustering Ideas   81
Strategies for Written Communication   81

✒ Situation 2: Freewriting 83
Strategies for Oral Communication 84
🗣 Situation 3: Assessing the Planning
of Oral Presentations 86
Summary 86
How to Approach a Selected Situation 87

6 Polishing Texts and Presentations 89
The Process of Revision 89
Eliminating Clutter 90
Revising on a Word Processor 92
The Importance of Proofreading 92
Strategies for Effective Proofreading 92
    The First Reading: Clarity and Sense 93
    The Second Reading: Line-by-Line Accuracy 93
    The Final Reading: Visual Impression 94
Proofreading with a Computer 94
    Spelling Checkers 94
    Grammar Checkers 95
Avoiding Common Grammar Errors 96
    Subject/Verb Agreement 96
    Pronoun/Antecedent Agreement 97
    Parallelism 98
Avoiding Sexist Usage 100
Assessing Page Layout 101
Polishing Oral Presentations 102
✒ Situation 1: Revising a Memo 102
🗣 Situation 2: Polishing an Oral Presentation 108
Summary 108
How to Approach a Selected Situation 109

PART THREE
FOCUSED COMMUNICATION CONTEXTS 111

7 Contexts for Written Communication 113
Writing as a Process 113
Letters and Memoranda 114
    Business Letters: General Advice 114
    Business Letters: Specific Contexts 116
✒ Situation 1: Writing a Direct and an Indirect Letter 121
    Memoranda: General Advice 121

Memoranda: Specific Contexts   122
✒ *Situation 2: Writing Memos*   123
Proposals   123
   Proposals: General Advice   123
Reports   125
   Reports: General Advice   125
   Executive Summary   127
   Executive Summary: General Advice   128
Case Analyses   129
   Cases: General Advice   129
CPA or CMA Examinations   130
   Exam Essays: General Advice   133
Group Writing Projects   133
   Group Writing Projects: General Advice   134
Summary   135
How to Approach Selected Situations   137
Appendix: Professional Examination
   Questions and Answers   139
   Uniform CPA Examination   139
   Certified Management Accountant Examination   142

8 Contexts for Oral Communication   **149**
Communication Apprehension: Nervousness Is Normal   150
   What to Know and Understand About
      Communication Apprehension   151
   What to Do About Communication Apprehension   152
💬 *Situation 1: Analyzing Communication Apprehension*   155
Presentations Versus Speeches   155
Presentation Contexts: Individual and Group   156
   Individual Presentations   156
💬 *Situation 2: Analyzing an Oral Presentation*   161
   Group Presentations   161
Interviews to Gather Information   163
   Preparation   164
   Questions and the Interview Schedule   165
   Listening   167
   Remembering and Recording   169
💬 *Situation 3: Practicing an Interview*   171
Summary   171
How to Approach a Selected Situation   173

Topical Table of Contents

(Chapter and page number in parentheses)

Analysis (1.7)
Analysis Versus Description (4.54) (7.129)
Appendixes (7.127)
Approach (4.54)
Audience Analysis (2.24) (2.27) (2.29) (3.39) (3.45) (5.78) (7.123) (7.125)
Audience-Centered Texts (3.38)
Audiotaping (5.83) (8.170)
Authoritative Pronouncements (4.66)
Avoiding Sexist Usage (6.100)
"Bad News" Letters (7.116)
Bar Graphs (4.68)
Brainstorming (5.80)
Cases (7.129)
Cause-Effect (Effect-Cause) Organization (4.61)
Chronological Organization (4.60)
Citations (4.63)
Clustering (5.80)
Common Grammar Errors (6.96)
Communication Apprehension (8.150)
Communication Contexts (2.23) (2.31)
Communication Plan (2.23) (5.77) (7.113)
Computer Graphics (4.70)
Content Organization (2.23) (4.59)
Conversational Style (7.115)
CPA or CMA Examinations (7.130)
Critical Thinking and Communication (1.6)
Cultural Considerations (3.44) (8.157)
Decreasing Order of Importance (4.61)
Dedicated Graphics Packages (4.71)

Delayed Notetaking (8.170)
Differences Between Written and Oral Communication (2.29)
Direct Approach (4.57) (7.117)
Drafting as Experimenting (5.79) (7.113)
Drafting: Getting Started (5.79)
Eliminating Clutter (6.90) (7.115)
Empathy (8.168)
Executive Summaries (4.62) (7.126) (7.127)
Extemporaneous Speaking (2.33) (5.85) (8.156)
Figures (4.68)
Formal Approach (4.55)
Freewriting (5.82)
"Good News" Letters (7.116)
Governmental Data (4.66)
Grammar Checkers (6.95)
Graphics (4.66) (6.105) (7.124)
Group Presentations (8.161)
Group Writing Projects (7.133)
Headings (7.123) (7.126) (7.129)
Impromptu Speaking (2.33)
Increasing Order of Importance (4.60)
Indirect Approach (7.117)
Individual Presentations (8.156)
Industry Data (4.65)
Informal Approach (4.55)
Information Sources (4.65)
Integrated Software Packages (4.71)
Interactive Communication (2.21)
Interview Schedule (8.165)
Interviewing (8.163)
Jargon (3.42) (8.165)
Letters (7.114)
Letters of Persuasion (7.118)
Letters of Request (7.118)
Line Graphs (4.68)
Listening (8.167)
Memoranda (7.114)
Multiple Audience (3.40)
Necessary Communication Skills (1.8)

Nonverbal Responses (3.46) (8.157)
Notetaking (8.169)
Objectives (2.30)
Organizational (Corporate) Culture (2.26)
Outline/Transition Form (5.79)
Page Layout (6.101)
Parallel Structure (6.98)
Paraphrasing and Quoting (4.63)
Physical Context (2.26)
Pictograms (4.69)
Pie Charts (4.69)
Plagiarism (4.64)
Prepositional Phrases (6.96)
Presentation Software (4.71)
Presentations Versus Speeches (8.155)
Probe Questions (8.166)
Professional and Academic Studies (4.66)
Pronoun/Antecedent Agreement (6.97)
Proofreading (6.92) (7.114)
Proofreading with a Computer (6.94)
Proposals (6.101) (7.123)
Publicly Available Data (4.65)
Purpose (2.24)
Question and Answer Style (6.106)
Reactive Thinking (1.8)
Reports (6.101) (7.125)
Revising on a Word Processor (6.92)
Revision (6.89) (7.113)
Role (2.24) (2.25)
Role of Accountants (1.4) (2.21) (2.25)
Role of Audience in Communication (3.37)
Roles in Organizational Context (2.26)
Semantics (6.104)
Single Audience (3.40)
Spelling Checkers (6.94)
Spreadsheets (4.70)
Storytelling Style (5.85)
Strategies for Clear Thinking (1.7)
Subject/Verb Agreement (6.96)

Summaries (4.62)
Surface Conventions (3.45) (5.83)
Synthesis (1.7) (4.63)
Table of Contents (Reports) (7.126)
Tables (4.67)
Target Audience (3.41)
Tax Regulations (4.66)
The Three S's (4.59)
Three-Step Method of Proofreading (6.92)
Title Page (Reports) (7.126)
Tone (7.115)
Topical Organization (4.60)
Traditional Model of Communication (2.20)
Types of Communication (1.5)
Unknown Audience (3.40)
Ways Accountants Communicate (1.4)
White Space (6.101)
Writer-Centered Texts (3.38)
Writing Process (7.113)

INTRODUCTION
Accounting and Communication

1
Communicating in Accounting

Imagine you have been asked to explain what accounting is to the following: a friend who has a liberal arts degree, a group of high school students on career day at the school, and a client who is an entrepreneur opening a restaurant. You have a sense of what you want to say, but you are faced with a series of decisions regarding your role, the audience you are addressing, the task at hand, and the ways you will communicate your message. Some of the interactions will be informal, while some should be formal. Choices have to be made about what should be stated orally and what should be put in writing. Within both oral and written presentations, there are additional decisions about format (e.g., chart or graph form? outline form? fully developed paragraphs?). In this book we suggest strategies to help you make such communication decisions.

When explaining accounting to those outside the profession, you might not think to emphasize that accounting is communication. However, *accounting is the accumulation, analysis, and coordinated use of information; and the communication of relevant information to decision makers.*[1] As an accountant you may communicate with current or potential stockholders, financial analysts, banks or other financial institutions, public accountants, and internal managers among others. Your audiences can include very knowledgeable people who understand technical jargon as well as those who are less informed and who need information presented in plain English. In addition, your communication involves both sending and receiving messages, eliciting and presenting information, and choosing what oral or written formats are appropriate.

This book integrates material dealing with the many dimensions of communication including working alone or in groups. By considering all these issues together, you will be better able to develop your own style for communication. In addition, accountants should value aspects of professional communication that are often neglected: reading, listening, and nonverbal sensitivity. Finally, many books and articles advise or give tips and techniques to try. This book goes beyond simple techniques to provide a more complete communication framework with

---

[1] While much of accounting deals with financial information, it's too limiting to narrow this definition to just financial information.

which to achieve greater success in communication. In this chapter you will consider: (1) the relationship between accounting and communication, (2) types of communication, (3) the link between thinking and communication, and (4) what skills are necessary to be able to communicate effectively.

Communication: The Core of Accounting

Accountants are both preparers and users of information. Information is news; it is useful to a decision maker and reduces uncertainty about the environment. As a preparer of information, you might be writing notes to accompany financial statements, interpreting auditing standards for a client, communicating with the Internal Revenue Service about a tax question, developing a new company's business plan that will go to lending institutions, or presenting an analysis of a possible capital asset acquisition to operating managers. Thus, communicating can involve all aspects of accounting (financial, managerial, tax, auditing, and systems) addressed to people who are either internal or external to the organization. Accountants can be part of the management team or can be consultants to management. In all cases, though, it is your responsibility to communicate effectively and efficiently with your audience, given the task at hand.

Role of Accountants

In the past, accountants might have seen their role merely as advisors, in staff rather than line positions. In such positions, all that is required is to present information and leave it to others to interpret and make decisions. For example, the father of one of the authors was an accountant during the 1950s at Ford Motor Company. Accounting personnel at his plant were expected to prepare reports for others to use and explain. They were not at management meetings; they were isolated from operations. In their careers, they might have never written a memorandum other than a technical note for the files. They were seen as number crunchers. This role has changed quite a bit over the years. Operating managers are telling accountants that they want not only "the figures," but also a complete analysis. In addition, managers might expect accounting personnel to participate in operating decisions. Thus, accountants both prepare and use information as an integral part of the management decision-making team.

Ways We Can Communicate

In some sense, modern life is plagued by too many communication choices. You can generate hard copies of letters, memoranda, and spreadsheets; send electronic mail to be viewed on a screen; record voice mail messages; produce videocassettes; have direct phone conversations; and meet one-on-one or in groups either formally or informally, in unmediated or mediated situations. To gather information, you have the same sources plus access to international data banks and highly specialized library documents. When presenting and eliciting information, you make many choices. This book will develop a framework for communication so that your choices are both more informed and explicit.

Types of Communication

You are the Chief Financial Officer of a new company that is going to buy an ongoing manufacturing business from its current owners. Over the last few months you have been working with several banks and other financial institutions to finance the start-up of the company. This involves buying the firm from its existing owners and developing funds for capital expansion and for working capital. You are at the point where two financial institutions have presented offers to your company. Neither is a perfect fit and there are tradeoffs between them as well as many points to be negotiated before a final decision is made. You are now deciding what information the Finance Committee of the new company's Board of Directors should have and how to communicate it. This committee is comprised of the Chairperson of the Board (a major investor with a service industry background), the President (currently in charge of the company that your new firm will be buying), and two members of the union that represents the workers in the plant.

Consider the choices that you have in this situation. You can present financial information in summary or in detail and in tabular or graphic form with or without accompanying notes. You can hand out copies of information and/or use overhead transparencies or computer-generated slides. Some information can be written and some can be spoken. You must also decide how technical you want to be. You have to focus on a primary objective of the presentation: making a decision today; introducing the issues to the audience; or persuading the Board to accept your own conclusions.

This problem illustrates the multiplicity of communication choices in accounting. Your options include communicating in writing or orally,[2]

---

[2] When we discuss *written communication*, we include any form of communication that involves creating a text to be read by the audience. It might be a handwritten letter, a computer-generated memorandum, or electronic mail. *Oral* or *speech communication* includes not only face-to-face situations, but also many electronically mediated messages, even those in which the communicators are removed from each other in time and space. Oral communication is usually direct interpersonal talk, but also could include teleconferencing, training videos, messages on telephone answering machines, and telephone calls. Many accounting tasks involve a combination of written and oral messages.

formally or informally, and verbally or nonverbally. You might be communicating with an individual or with a group. You might be listening/receiving, actively eliciting information, or presenting it to others. You must make informed and explicit choices about how you are communicating. Your goal is to develop communication that works best for all the parties concerned.

Critical Thinking and Communication: An Inseparable Combination

As we have just shown, all communication involves choosing among available options. Making these choices requires critical thinking.[3] In written communication, for example, you start out with a blank piece of paper or computer screen. You create text through a series of choices—words, sentences, paragraphs, format. You are in basic control of the decision-making process, but the choices you make depend on a string of variables—purpose, intended audience, your role, and context. In writing this book, we had to think through these dimensions and keep rethinking them as each word, sentence, paragraph, and chapter was written. By becoming aware of the full range of decisions to be made, you are less likely to be trapped in oversimplified assumptions. Understanding how complex communication can be actually makes it less threatening and intimidating.

Many people fear or dislike writing, for example. If you are one of them, it may help you to consider that as a writer, you have complete control over the creation (writing) process. No one will know how many drafts you wrote; no one will be aware of the number of times you rewrote your first sentence. Knowing you have control can be an overwhelming responsibility, but it can also be empowering.

People who have good critical thinking skills must realize that substance (the result of their analysis) is inseparable from the form of communication. When you are communicating, critical thinking is an integral part of that process; however, good critical thinking is useless if the results of that analysis cannot be communicated to others. In the same regard, something that is grammatically correct and contains all the right buzz words but lacks any depth of analysis is equally useless to managers who want information for decision making. It is false to assume that written English (grammar, spelling, punctuation, etc.) or interpersonal speech (language choices, eye contact, voice inflection, etc.) are separate from content. Our view is that critical thinking and communication are inseparable.

---

[3] Critical thinking is the process of systematically investigating and evaluating alternatives for solving problems. It involves both analysis (separating a problem into its component parts) and synthesis skills (recognizing how the parts of a problem relate together as a whole).

Situation 1: Assessing an Assignment

You are a teacher and have decided to assign an essay where students will analyze and critique two books they were asked to read. A student hands in a paper that has no errors in grammar and usage, but is only a description of the books' contents. On a scale of 0 to 10, how would you rate this paper? Explain your rationale for the rating.

Strategies for Clear Thinking

Effective thinking does not come automatically. Applying the following strategies to your communication contexts will enable you to develop a well-thought-out communication plan.

1. *Focus on the problem or task.* Before you can analyze a situation, you need to free yourself from outside distractions and concentrate on the task at hand. Put yourself in an environment that is conducive to uninterrupted thinking. This might mean completing other tasks (e.g., returning telephone calls, paying bills) before starting.

2. *Determine your goals or objectives.* Part of the skill of focusing is defining your problem clearly and accurately. What, specifically, needs to be addressed? Decide what exactly you are hoping to accomplish. If you are not clear about your goals, then you have no way of developing a meaningful strategy and no way of assessing the eventual outcome. For example, in the preceding illustration, the CFO had to determine the objective of the presentation before deciding how to communicate information to the Finance Committee.

3. *Consider the big picture.* Too many people do not stop to think about all the factors that make up any given situation: e.g., how does my decision here affect others? If you narrow your viewpoint too much, you may miss important aspects which may have relevance to the final outcome. Effective problem-solvers remember that both analysis (separating a problem into its component parts) and synthesis (acknowledging the links between seemingly separate issues) are crucial.

4. *Follow each idea or solution to its logical conclusions.* For every idea you develop, you need to take the next step and ask yourself, "If I do this, what will be the likely outcome?" Actions have consequences; thus, any decision you make needs to be considered with an eye on the probable results.

5. *Consider each idea from an alternative angle or point of view.* By putting yourself in the place of another person, you can often see a situation totally differently. If you were the intended audience, what would you think and how would you feel? This alternative viewpoint can help you to better assess the problem or situation and may even help you to arrive at a more acceptable solution.

6. *Avoid reactive thinking.* When you make a split-second judgment or decision without considering the ramifications of your actions, you are guilty of reactive thinking, thinking that comes strictly as a reaction to a problem. For example, you might feel pressure from your supervisor or teacher, so you take some action to relieve the pressure. Reactive thinking may lead to solutions that work in the short run, but often this type of thinking can cause long-term problems because time was not taken to carefully assess the likely aftermath of the action.

7. *Take a break before the final assessment of your ideas and solutions.* You will be able to make clearer judgments about your ideas if you put the work aside for a period of time. This gives your brain a break and allows you to return to the problem with a fresher, more objective outlook. If possible, give yourself a day or two before you go back to assess your ideas a final time. If your schedule does not allow you the luxury of a day, then take a break and allow yourself to think of other things before returning to your task.

Clear thinking is the first step to clear communication.

Situation 2: Thinking Through a Task

Your boss comes into your office and says, "I just returned from a meeting where they talked about how we could save money by doing our own tax returns rather than having an outsider do them. I want you to prepare a presentation for senior management to explore and explain this idea."

Use the preceding steps to plan an approach to this request.

Necessary Communication Skills

For many years practitioners have been sending a strong message to those who are about to enter the profession: technical accounting skills are not enough; accountants must be able to communicate effectively through both writing and speaking. Thirty percent of the accounting firms surveyed by *The Wall Street Journal*[4] reported dissatisfaction with the communication skills of entry-level accountants. Another study[5] cited poor writing skills as a major reason for job terminations among entry-level accountants. Stout et al.[6] report that practicing CMAs place great importance on communication skills (speaking, writing, and listening). Novin and Pearson[7] surveyed partners in CPA firms to find out, among other things, the skills these partners thought were necessary for entry-level public accountants. Novin et al.[8] sought the same information regarding entry-level management accountants from controllers of United States corporations who are CMAs. Respondents to these two studies thought the following skills were either very important or extremely important for entry-level accountants:

	CPA Partners	CMA Controllers
Thinking skills	96%	95%
Problem-solving skills	95%	97%
Listening skills	92%	91%
Writing skills	89%	92%
Speaking skills	77%	49%

Novin et al. conclude that:

> Writing, listening, verbal, and overall management skills were identified as either important skills ... or as current weaknesses.... The need for these skills indicates that more practice in public speaking, writing, and group discussion is warranted in all phases of the accounting curriculum.[9]

The need for better communication and critical thinking skills is also called for in the report of the American Accounting Association Committee on the Future, Structure, Content, and Scope of Accounting Education (the Bedford Committee),[10] by the (then) Big Eight Account-

---

[4] S. Feinstein, "Words Count." *The Wall Street Journal* (July 15, 1986): 1, 5.

[5] *Management Accounting Campus Report*, May 1989 (Montvale, NJ: Institute of Management Accountants).

[6] D. Stout, D. Wygal, and K. Hoff, "Writing Across the Disciplines: Applications to the Accounting Classroom." *The Bulletin of the Association for Business Communication* 53.4 (1990): 10–16.

[7] A. Novin and M. Pearson, "Non-Accounting Knowledge Qualifications for Entry-Level Public Accountants." *The Ohio CPA Journal* (Winter 1989): 12–17.

[8] A. Novin, M. Pearson, and S. Senge, "Improving the Curriculum for Aspiring Management Accountants: The Practitioner's Point of View." *Journal of Accounting Education* 8 (1990): 207–224.

[9] Novin et al., 220.

[10] American Accounting Association [AAA] Committee on the Future Structure, Content, and Scope of Accounting Education, "Future Accounting Education: Preparing for the Expanding Profession." *Issues in Accounting Education* 1 (1990): 168–195.

ing firms[11] and by the Accounting Education Change Commission (AECC).[12] The Big Eight statement on accounting education claims:

> Public accounting requires its practitioners to be able to transfer and receive information with ease.
>
> Practitioners must be able to present and defend their views through formal and informal, written and oral, presentation. They must be able to do so at a peer level with business executives.[13]

The AECC states:

> To become successful professionals, accounting graduates must possess communication skills.... Communication skills include both receiving and transmitting information and concepts, including effective reading, listening, writing, and speaking.[14]

Among other things, in order to become skilled in communication and successful in accounting, you have to work on thinking, writing, reading, speaking, and listening. Technical competence is just the first step to accounting success. Even if you can communicate effectively through writing, if you cannot be an active participant in a problem-solving discussion with your peers and/or supervisor or are unable to address a large group, you have limited your own growth and potential. Others at the organization at which you work will notice, too, how you are limiting the organization.

It's scary to think about all these skills. Certainly most of us are more comfortable with a particular style of communicating such as informal conversation or creating computer spreadsheets. Most of us will never be equally comfortable with all the dimensions of communication. Some will like public speaking, while others will hate it. Some will like writing lengthy analyses, while others will cringe at the thought. As stated before, the objective here is to put you more in control of your own destiny and direction. While you might not develop excellent skill levels in all the areas explored in this book, you will at least be more relaxed and competent if you follow these guidelines.

---

[11] Arthur Andersen & Co., Arthur Young, Coopers & Lybrand, Deloitte Haskins & Sells, Ernst & Whinney, Peat Marwick Main & Co., Price Waterhouse, and Touche Ross, *Perspectives on Education: Capabilities for Success in the Accounting Profession* (New York: Authors, 1989).

[12] Accounting Education Change Commission, "Objectives of Education for Accountants: Position Statement Number 1." *Issues in Accounting Education* 5 (1990): 307–312.

[13] Big Eight, 6.

[14] AECC, 307.

Basic Skills Assumed

If you are using this book in conjunction with a university course, we assume that you have taken basic English and speech communication classes. We also assume that you will use this book along with an appropriate reference writing/style manual. Therefore, we will concentrate on the larger issues that affect practicing accountants in addition to basic language conventions such as grammar and punctuation.

You Must Be an Active Learner

We want to engage you directly in the learning process. Each chapter includes practical, viable strategies and suggestions that reflect our recognition of what accountants actually *do*. You can apply the concepts both in course work and on the job. You can use this book as an organized program of study by reading through it from beginning to end, and you can also use it for troubleshooting by investigating specific answers to questions and problems you encounter. It is important to see that we are not proposing mere theory here or something that you can gain only through "book learning." Becoming skilled in communication involves ongoing practice so that competence becomes second nature.

What's Included in This Book

The book is divided into three major sections. In Part One we deal with developing a communication plan. Chapter 2 describes how to analyze the context and purpose, establishing the idea that all communication involves coordinating roles, audiences, and tasks. Communication is not just a neat sequence of information transfer, but a delicate process of collaboration. Chapter 3 emphasizes the importance of analyzing your audience as you prepare to communicate. Chapter 4 helps you develop your actual content. Part Two of the book involves implementing a communication plan. Chapters 5 and 6 discuss how to create (draft) a persuasive text and polish it through editing and revising. Finally, Part Three applies these practical ideas to focused communication contexts. Chapter 7 suggests strategies for writing memoranda, letters, proposals, reports, cases, professional examinations, and group writing projects. Chapter 8 presents special oral communication challenges, including stage fright, presentations, interviews, and group presentations. Except for the last two chapters that analyze special problems associated with written or oral communication formats, all other chapters include relevant elements of both formats and discuss listening and eliciting of information as well.

Summary

Accounting involves the sharing of relevant information and interpretations among decision makers. As managers or accounting-related professionals, you are faced with many choices on how to communicate effectively given your role, the audience you are addressing, and the task at hand. You might be more comfortable with some ways of communicating than with others. However, by taking a critical look at how to communicate better orally and in writing, formally and informally, to individuals and to groups, and by developing listening and information elicitation skills, you can increase your chances for success and for control over your career.

How to Approach Selected Situations

Situation 1: Assessing an Assignment

The important words in this assignment are *analyze* and *critique*. Analysis requires that you go beyond merely describing the content; you need to view the content in terms of its relevance to a particular context or a particular set of criteria. Criticism involves offering a review of the content; you need to look at the strengths and weaknesses of the text. Therefore, a paper that is free from surface errors in grammar and usage but does not analyze or criticize the two books is not fulfilling the assignment.

Some teachers would be hard pressed to give any credit at all for an essay that clearly does not meet the terms of an assignment. They'd define the situation as one of principle in which there is little opportunity for choice. A "0" would be the rating earned by the student. You would be justified in assigning it if you were the teacher, and the student—learning this lesson—might give the next task much more attention.

However, thinking analytically might make you consider the assignment and the student's response to it as itself an opportunity for problem-solving and analysis. Divide the problem, for example, into two parts—the demands of your role compared with the demands of the student's role. You know as a teacher that your role is to encourage and enable learning. You also understand (from this chapter and perhaps your own experience) that many people fear writing and they often believe that thorough description can substitute for analysis. Effective analysis goes beyond pointing to the content, and creatively tries to take a problem apart to see what makes it tick. In doing so, the student writer would learn to understand the books better by asking not just "what?" questions (emphasizing content), but "why?" questions (emphasizing deeper questions of causality and relationship). Taking all this into account, you may decide to give the otherwise successful paper partial credit (perhaps 2 to 4 points) and use this opportunity to reinforce the distinction between description and analysis without discouraging the student too much.

Situation 2: Thinking Through a Task

As with most of the hypothetical situations described in this book, the description doesn't give enough information for definitive answers. Therefore, instead of looking at a specific solution, use the details you do know about the boss' request to probe or test your understanding of the seven suggested critical thinking strategies.

First, defer the planning of your response if possible until you can give it your full attention. Second, in order to clarify your own goals, think carefully about the wording and presumed intent of the supervisor's request. Is he or she asking for a presentation that would *advocate* internal tax return preparation, or one that would simply *describe* the advantages and disadvantages of such a change? Once you know what you hope to accomplish, you can decide on the best format for your presentation. Third, place this single task in the "big picture" of the organization by asking yourself whose positions would be helped, harmed, changed, or bolstered by the changed procedures. You'd probably need specific data about how much is paid currently to outside preparers, how accurate their work has been, and the existing organizational expertise and potential resources available to commit to this task. Also consider short- versus long-term tradeoffs of the decision. This information will allow you to generate some alternative solutions to your task.

Fourth, anticipate possible outcomes of your alternative choices. For example, if you prepare a written executive summary comparison, what should be its length, and what are its chances of being read carefully? If you ask for a brief meeting to explain the alternatives to senior management, how likely are they to allot the time you need to do valid comparisons? Fifth, as much as possible, identify or empathize with the people who will be affected by who prepares the tax return, or who will implement the decision. Think about their concerns and what points they would think were important. Anticipating outcomes realistically and imagining reactions are excellent ways to begin to evaluate alternatives in problem-solving.

Strategies six and seven are checks on the process that could save you from rash decisions. Consider your own personality and previous work habits to make sure you don't jump to an early conclusion that barricades your judgment from otherwise effective solutions. For instance, your first *inner* reaction to the boss' statement might be "That's stupid. Why spread ourselves even thinner in this department when Talbot, Morslick have been doing such a great job on taxes?" This dismisses the suggestion too soon, and even though it's an internal reaction, it will affect subtly the commitment you feel to the presentation. In the same way, don't let the interest of your boss influence your thinking. Your job is to investigate; it's senior management's job to make final judgments. Don't confuse the two roles.

Finally, suppose you've decided to make a balanced presentation of the pros and cons of internal tax preparation. Once you have a sense of how you're going to proceed, put the project aside for awhile. When you come back to it, review your ideas and intended approach. You might have more or better ideas. Some of your strategies might look less promising. Make any revisions in your plan you think are necessary.

Obviously, these strategies won't necessarily make your presentation easier or magically make your decisions for you. They may, however, clarify matters enough to make your decisions more helpful to your organization.

Appendix: Suggested Background Material

If you believe that you need additional background in basic communication skills, refer to one or more of the following.

Writing and Reading

For basic skill guidance and inspiration in the field of written communication, you may want to refer to:

Adler, M. (1940). *How to Read a Book*. New York: Simon and Schuster. This is a classic description of what a reader can do to enhance communication with an author.

Elbow, P. (1973). *Writing Without Teachers*. London: Oxford University Press. A creative and entertaining book. Elbow justifies how each of us can become writers who are reader-centered.

Fuess, B., Jr. (Ed.). (1985). *How to Use the Power of the Printed Word*. Garden City, NY: Doubleday Anchor Press. The award-winning series of International Paper Company ads appeared in newspapers and national magazines in the early 1980s. It includes practical tips on punctuation, style, vocabulary, and other issues from such noted writers as Russell Baker, Erma Bombeck, John Irving, Jane Bryant Quinn, and Kurt Vonnegut.

Goldberg, N. (1986). *Writing Down the Bones: Freeing the Writer Within*. Boston: Shambhala. Do you get stuck or blocked as a writer? Goldberg's suggestions help you decide when, where, and in what mood to write, not just how to write.

Strunk, W., Jr., & White, E. B. (1979). *The Elements of Style* (3rd ed.). New York: Macmillan. This is the best-known guide to writing style. Although it adopts an authoritarian tone at times, many writers still swear by it.

Zinsser, W. (1988). *On Writing Well: An Informal Guide to Writing Nonfiction* (3rd ed.). New York: Harper and Row. Zinsser is considered a writer's writer. He includes especially effective discussions of editing, along with an excellent chapter on working with a word processor.

Speaking and Listening

The following sources provide excellent discussions of the basics of speaking and listening, especially in professional settings.

Bolton, R. (1979). *People Skills*. Englewood Cliffs, NJ: Prentice Hall. This is perhaps the best popularized introduction to the range and importance of interpersonal communication skills.

Borisoff, D., & Purdy, M. (1991). *Listening in Everyday Life: A Personal and Professional Approach*. Lanham, MD: University Press of America. A thorough and practical look at an often-neglected aspect of communication. This book will help you listen across differences of gender, culture, and value.

Doolittle, R. J. (1984). *Professional Speaking: A Concise Guide*. Glenview, IL: Scott, Foresman. A brief, no-frills introduction to making organizational presentations and conducting professional interviews.

Eisenberg, A. (1979). *Job Talk: Communicating Effectively on the Job*. New York: Macmillan. A longtime business communication consultant focuses on the informal factors that make or break communicators in their jobs. It includes many involving stories and concrete examples along with some self-assessment tools.

Hoff, R. (1988). *"I Can See You Naked": A Fearless Guide to Making Great Presentations*. Kansas City: Andrews and McMeel. Although this book has a silly title, it is amazingly practical. It includes excellent strategies for alleviating communication apprehension and stage fright.

Stone, J., & Bachner, J. (1977). *Speaking Up: A Book for Every Woman Who Wants to Speak Effectively*. New York: McGraw-Hill. An exploration of the special challenges and opportunities that women speakers face in organizational life.

PART ONE
Developing a Communication Plan

2
Analyzing Context and Purpose

Jim Smith, the new Director of Purchasing, was having trouble becoming acclimated at DynamiCo. Although his degree was from a prestigious university, and despite his rapid climb in the company, others still noticed that as a manager he was indecisive and slow to understand how decisions were made in the company. One day, while walking by another office, he overheard two co-workers talking about him: "Jim doesn't know what he's doing here." "That's for sure. Hope he gets with the program soon, or we're done for."

One of the most damaging comments that can be made about a manager or co-worker is that he (or she) doesn't know what he's doing. Whether it's said by workers about their supervisor or by the supervisor about the new salesperson, listeners seem to understand immediately that the problem is not necessarily one of skill deficiency, but of an inability to adapt to a particular context.

If you listen closely when this accusation is made, it's clear that only very rarely does the critic mean that the person does not know how to do his or her job. The basic techniques are often clearly understood; Jim knows the English language well enough to write a report, knows how to conduct a survey or an audit, has basic accounting skills, and knows computers backward and forward. However, "He doesn't know what he's doing." What can this suggest, if it doesn't refer to basic skill knowledge?

Such an organizational criticism usually points to the person's context blindness or ignorance. Jim has "know-how," but he has yet to learn when to apply it, how much of it to use, where to try it, who to show it to, and how to adapt his ideas for different people in the organization. In a sense, someone who doesn't know what he or she is doing is lost, just as surely as a lost traveler may still have a nearly full gas tank or shoe leather left, but lacks a clear-cut route to a destination. The "lost" feeling of context ignorance is essentially a communication problem. This chapter includes practical strategies to help you decide where you are relative to the audiences and destinations you need to reach. Assuming you have basic "know-how," it's time to think about the contextual *know-when, know-why,* and *know-where.*

19

In reading this chapter, you will consider: (1) a "both sides" alternative to the typical understanding of what constitutes communication, (2) the need to develop a tentative communication plan, (3) the influence of roles in analyzing any communication situation, (4) a comparison between writing and speaking modes in communication, and (5) specific strategies for adapting your goals to the different requirements of written and spoken communication.

Before we discuss specific strategies, let's expand the concept of communication introduced in Chapter 1. Although some may believe that communication is merely the accurate conveying of information or meaning from one person to another, this is a very limited view of the dynamics of communication.

Communication: Beyond Transmission

The Traditional Model

A noted organizational consultant used to ask (before gender-neutral language was common in everyday usage) business executives in his workshops to evaluate the following definition of communication:

> When Person X "communicates" with Person Y, what happens is that he transmits meanings (information, facts, ideas, etc.) from his mind to the mind of Person Y.[1]

In the discussion that followed his purposely inadequate definition, "virtually 100 percent" of the hundreds of executives he asked thought that such a definition was clear, succinct, and effective in defining the responsibilities of the business communication process.[2] After all, they must have reasoned, surely the business environment is one in which some people have the appropriate information and others don't. Thus those needing information receive the proper facts and ideas from those who possess information. This information transmission model is often taken by executives to be the natural way communication should work. Simplified somewhat in Figure 2–1, communication is understood by such persons as a transmission. However, negative effects from this top-down, one-way philosophy have stimulated more recent recommendations for increased "people skills" in business education, as reported in an influential national research study.[3]

---

[1] W. Redding, "Human Communication Behavior in Complex Organizations: Some Fallacies Revisited." In C. Larson & F. Dance (Eds.), *Perspectives on Communication* (Milwaukee, WI: Speech Communication Center, University of Wisconsin, 1968), pp. 99–112.

[2] Redding, 101.

[3] L. Porter & L. McKibbon, *Management Education and Development: Drift or Thrust into the 21st Century* (New York: McGraw Hill, 1988).

Figure 2–1. Transmission of Information

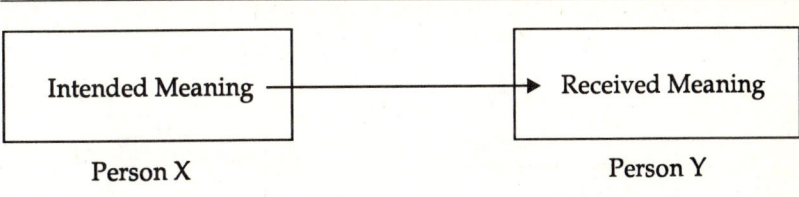

```
┌─────────────────────┐
│  Intended Meaning   │─────────▶   Received Meaning
└─────────────────────┘

       Person X                         Person Y
```

Interactive Communication

The guiding notion of the workshop in which these executives were participating was very different from the traditional transmission model explained previously. Human communication, they discovered, is essentially a mutual experience in which all parties in the process simultaneously influence the other(s). Thus, a meaning for a message doesn't start with the sender who deposits it within the receiver. Instead, meaning is uniquely created (in a sense, built or constructed) in the interaction between the communicators. In addition, the meaning between any two communicators will necessarily differ when compared to any other communicators, even if the content of the communication is exactly the same. If you receive a message regarding some problems with the corporate tax return, your interpretation will be different if it came from a colleague rather than an IRS examiner. This is an interactive view of communication that stresses the importance of meanings that the communicators build together.

By **communication** we mean the process by which humans interact with messages to structure and make sense of any situation. Such communication may be verbal and symbolic (such as writing/reading or speaking/listening), or it may be nonverbal and behavioral (such as interpreting posture, gestures, voice tone, or how much time your boss allots for lunch).

Figure 2–2 shows a diagram of the interactive approach to communication. Although it's slightly more complicated than Figure 2–1, it can help you anticipate a wider range of realistic communication problems. Instead of just a one-way message, Figure 2–2 shows that meaning is based on the interaction of the sender and receiver given the history, skills, and style of each; the relationship between them; the interpretation and feedback each gives; and the context of the message.

As you plan your communications, keep in mind that it is an interactive process. This has the following implications for organizational communicators:

1. *The Both-Sides Issue.* Your readers and listeners are just as important in determining the ultimate meaning of your communication as you are as writer or speaker. When we are listeners or readers, we can

Figure 2–2. Interactive Communication

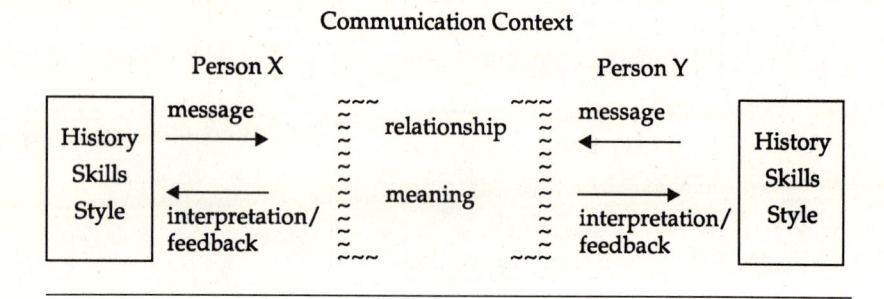

Communication Context

Person X			Person Y	
History Skills Style	message → ← interpretation/ feedback	relationship meaning	message ← interpretation/ → feedback	History Skills Style

examine the effectiveness of the message. Using this perspective, you can improve your ability to send messages to others. For example, if you receive a report on how a certain financial accounting rule is being applied at your firm, besides just reading the report, you can use this as an opportunity to see what you think is useful and not useful in the communication. How would you have done it differently? What are its strengths? You can use this analysis to help you improve your own writing ability.

2. *The Relationship Issue.* A single message you send can have vastly different meanings for different persons, depending on their previous experience, their relation to the source, the communication setting, and many other contextual factors. The message neither carries nor creates meaning; meaning is created out of the relationship between person(s) and message(s). Junior staff accountants are accustomed to receiving messages evaluating their work from senior staff and managers. If they received a similar message directly from a partner, it would probably have a different meaning.

3. *The Interpretation Issue.* When you communicate, your listener or reader may create private inner meanings to give tentative meaning to your actions. This is a shadow dimension of communication that has little to do with a speaker or writer's intent. Whatever you intend to say, or even if you intend to say literally nothing, others will interpret your words, posture, letterhead, timing, and even your silence or absence. You may not think anything is being communicated, but on the shadow side of communication, meaning is quietly being built. The silent stare of a CEO or the tone of how an employee is summoned by a supervisor is inevitably interpreted by the employee; that interpretation might or might not match what was intended by that look or tone of voice.

4. *The Creativity Issue.* Writers and speakers often aren't aware of what they need to communicate until they encounter an audience. Thus, you might come prepared to discuss some topic, but find that it is more

important to deal with another, more basic one. The traditional model of communication transmission implies that the writer or speaker already knows what he or she wants to say, and that the audience will (or should) receive that prepackaged message. However, communication is not simply the expression of predetermined meanings; it's the creative process of discovering together with an audience what you, and they, know and can know. Obviously, you often need to have your intentions understood. Communication planning is a goal-directed activity in which we try to accomplish certain objectives. However, you shouldn't be so concerned with following plans that you inhibit the natural creative potential of communication, which is collaboration.

5. *The Context Issue.* You can make almost any statement in such a way that negates its literal content. Imagine the first day of your new job, as you dress for success. You ask a friend or your spouse, "How do I look?" The reply is: "Oh . . . you're going to wear that? Interesting choice." Although the dictionary definitions of these words are clear enough to you, the face value of the total message cannot be separated from its context. Context awareness is the basis of irony, of friendly kidding, of sarcasm, of subtle suggestion and sly digs, and of social tact as well. If you're context blind, you may feel complimented when the speaker intended no such thing, or feel put down when he or she thought you were hearing positive feedback. Effective communicators also interpret, among other things, the tone of voice, the statement's placement in the flow of a conversation, the history of communication habits and preferences of your partner, and the immediate context. Without an awareness of such clues, the dictionary meanings of the words will not help communicators much. The importance of context is the reason why it is inadvisable to offer a collection of communication rules and prescriptions to new accounting professionals. Though rules may sometimes help, they do not really teach the learner to be flexible in encountering new situations.

With these basic concepts in mind, let's explore how to plan for effective communication.

Developing a Communication Plan

The first step toward effective communication is to create a communication plan: a tentative design for action. Trying to create a written report or an oral presentation without some sort of plan is like trying to prepare tax forms without knowing the IRS regulations. A communication plan helps you to focus on your goals as a communicator and also serves as a guide and point of reference for you to use as you draft and revise your message. The four main components of a communication plan are:

1. *Purpose.* Establish what you hope to accomplish within a communication situation, and how you can best meet these objectives. For example, if you are dealing with an operational audit of a quality problem in the plant, consider whether you want to lay out information you have discovered, give options for solving the problem, and/or make specific recommendations.

2. *Role Analysis.* Define your role within this specific communication situation. You might be internal (a member of the organization) or external (someone from outside the organization). Some examples later in the chapter show that your role affects what you want to say and how you want to say it.

3. *Audience Analysis.* Determine who will be receiving the message. This means thinking about their goals; their responsibilities; their beliefs, attitudes, and values; and what motivates them to communicate as they do. Chapter 3 discusses this in detail.

4. *Content Framework.* Plan how you can frame the message to meet the audience's needs and expectations. Assess what you have to say and whether you have researched the topic thoroughly enough to request readers' or listeners' time and careful attention. Plan how you will organize your information. For example, having an hour to present some ideas about new trends in manufacturing accounting in an informal meeting within your department is a different challenge than having fifteen minutes to brief the company president on the same subject. Surely you wouldn't tell the president, "No, thank you; I'd need at least an hour of your time to summarize these complex changes adequately." Instead, you would try to frame the content to fit the task at hand.

Each of these components will be considered in detail in this and in subsequent chapters.

Creating an effective communication plan may involve developing a detailed outline, making extensive notes, and researching audience background. On the other hand, your planning may have to occur with only a few minutes of thought and only a few notes or reminders. The complexity of a communication plan and the time needed to create it are determined by the time frame within which you're working and the complexity of the communication itself. Planning a brief memo may take only a few minutes of thought, while planning a detailed analysis of a tax question may involve several weeks of research and planning.

Many busy accountants make the mistake of thinking there is no time to create a communication plan. They want to get right to the report itself and avoid what they see as an unnecessary waste of time. Communication developed without careful planning, though pleasant in some informal situations, often lacks focus or direction in professional contexts. Without a clear plan, you may lose sight of your goals; you may create a message that is useless for your intended audience; or you may leave out important ideas and information. Careful planning allows you to think through the entire context so that, unlike Jim in the opening example of this chapter, you will "know what you're doing."

Communicator Roles

People might think of roles as being played by actors on a stage, in movies, or on television with scripted and predetermined interactions among the players. However, in most social situations, people assume roles and anticipate each other's actions. Here, role means those behaviors and communication habits that audiences and communicators come to expect of a particular person in a particular context. Normally, a person's objective in a given situation determines to some extent his or her role. For example, if you want a group to change its policies, you may adopt a leadership role in order to persuade rather than taking on a role of passive observer simply to acquiesce to other members' wishes. You might assume the role of teacher when you help others obtain information. Other common roles are facilitator, catalyst, mediator, negotiator, supervisor, confidant, parent, and so forth. Each role has customary and expected behaviors associated with it; leaders, for instance, are expected in Western culture to be relatively active, decisive, and talkative, while mediators are expected to be overtly unbiased in their choice of language.

Roles and the implicit rules that accompany them don't prescribe exactly what should happen in interaction, but they do tend to enclose people within some boundaries for behavior that is socially acceptable. You need to be both *role-sensitive* and *role-flexible* at the same time to be an effective communicator. Be sensitive to the role implications of a given situation, and flexible with your role to meet the expectations of listeners or readers. You must meet enough of the role expectations of your audience so they will perceive you as credible (expert and trustworthy in the given task), but you can't be locked into a straitjacket of expectations that eliminate your personal style.

Accountants' Roles

As an accountant, you are expected to perform many specific roles, including statistician, decision maker, investigator, advisor, observer, and questioner. Your technical roles within the organization will often be quite specialized and, to some extent, arbitrarily chosen by superiors. Yet your responsibilities will create an impact far beyond their obvious influence. For instance, you might be on a team of accountants that is asked by management to work independently to produce a report concerning whether the company will purchase and maintain its own fleet of cars, or continue to lease through commercial agencies. Your team might choose to adopt a neutral, objective, and scientific stance and present a set of facts with no recommendations. Alternatively, the team could act as advocates and recommend a course of action they believe is justified by the data. Your team can explain, as teachers might, or lead and persuade, as salespersons might. The differences, as you will see in later chapters, are crucial. What gives you credibility as an objective researcher may not increase your credibility in an advocacy role. The messages you'll send to your audience will be necessarily different.

In this situation, it is also important to consider how your team's roles are defined by others. Will the team be seen by the board as consultants to be questioned by board members who disagree—or as mouthpieces for the executive who gave you the task in the first place?

Roles in Organizational Context

An accountant's role makes a significant difference in how a report should be written and circulated in the first place. Roles make rules, and rules make or break people in organizations. Here are seven practical guidelines for making contextual role decisions in organizations:

1. *Analyze the organizational culture.* Examine the norms, the ways of talking, the customary topics, the recurring stories, and the dramatic tensions of the group. Some would call this an **organizational** or **corporate culture**, by analogy to the differences between ethnic and national cultures. What will work in a Japanese company will not be effective at the Kansas City Brass Works. Additionally, Kansas City Brass Works and its culture cannot be directly translated to Mutual of Omaha's corporate culture. A joke heard as witty in one office may be considered gauche and tasteless in another.

2. *Analyze the physical context.* Think about where you will be communicating your ideas and listening to others. It might be in an auditorium with audiovisual facilities, or in a small conference room with a circular table. All other things being equal, an auditorium invites a more formal presentational style, while a small conference room encourages feedback, discussion, and interchange of ideas among audience members. If you are insensitive to the constraints of the physical environment you will be a less effective communicator.

Physical context can also have an impact on written communication. Simply ask yourself such questions as: Where will my report likely be read? What else is likely to be distracting the reader while he or she considers my ideas, and how can I allow for these distractions? For example, in one office, workers noticed that a manager carried her morning mail around with her and read it while she made the rounds to visit different department heads. This might affect the complexity and elaboration of the reasoning you use in a memo to her. You could suggest a follow-up appointment with her to explain key passages.

3. *Analyze your audience's investment.* In other words, determine who (within the context in which you work) has a stake in what outcome. In our previous automobile fleet example, some employees may feel that their personal prestige with their clients is enhanced when they lease an expensive new car each year, and fear that company ownership might mean that company-owned cars would likely be subcompacts that would be replaced only after several years of wear and tear. No matter how intelligent and objective a report might be, it will always be read through the subjective filters of such personal involvement. Similarly, the executive who commissioned the study may be projecting/protecting a personal image as an innovator, a cost-conscious manager, or an ally of the CEO. The study may be perceived as an extension of that image, and the team should take that fact into account. Unfortunately, such role complications are often not anticipated and the chances for effective communication diminish.

4. *Analyze audience characteristics.* This is a small-scale version of how survey researchers discover the relevant social and demographic characteristics of a group of consumers or voters. A demographic profile is not foolproof, but it goes a long way toward helping communicators predict the issues, styles, roles, and strategies that would be most appropriate for a given audience. When an advertising agency buys commercial time on *Saturday Night Live*, it has access to the network's demographic research. It knows the age, gender, racial makeup, mean income, purchasing habits, and average impulse spending habits of the viewership. It's no accident that the resulting commercial appeals in a consistent way to the values suggested by such consumption groups. If you ultimately find the commercial irritating, you might be tempted to call the whole process manipulative, but advertisers simply defend it as a coordinated system of communication in which an audience as a whole is more likely to gain access to the information and products it wants. In the same way, it is not necessarily unethical or manipulative for you to provide information that is well adapted to audience needs, habits, listening styles, and goals. Chapter 3 discusses audience analysis and focuses specifically on this crucial communication problem.

5. *Analyze your personal investment.* You might have strong feelings about or feel ego-involved in the ideas you will be explaining; you might be unable to hear or unwilling to consider alternate interpretations and disagreements with your point of view. Do you tend to see suggestions, objections, and modifications as confrontations, as nitpicking, or as subversions of your good efforts? Unfortunately, many communicators unwittingly take revision as rejection. A healthier perspective is to un-

derstand that your message is not itself a final product, but a contribution toward a productive exchange of ideas.

6. *Analyze your personal strengths.* Consider whether you have been more successful in writing situations or in speaking situations. Look at whether you are more successful with an expansive expository writing style or with a more concise summary style. You may have had different kinds of success with formal public speaking, or informal conversational dialogue. If necessary, interview friends and co-workers you trust to provide you with reliable and honest feedback. If you have a choice in the form, format, or context of your communication, you can use this assessment as a basis for your choices. Of course, books such as this one seek to expand your repertoire so that ideally you'll be flexible enough to communicate in a style appropriate to any given audience or context.

7. *Analyze your communication plan from an audience perspective.* Understanding communication as an interactive process means that you see a speaker or a writer's power to influence audiences, but you also recognize the power of the audience. It's especially important, given this interdependence, to decide what you want to *accomplish with* (not *do to*) the audience. You have to decide if you want to inform the audience, persuade them to alter their attitudes, coordinate your goals and needs with theirs, motivate them, entertain them, or some focused combination of these.

Situation 1: Writing Memos Based on Roles

The president of a chain of pharmacies wants a recommendation (in memo form) about whether the company should drop the sale of cosmetics.

1. What information would you want before writing your memo?

2. How would your memorandum differ if there were the following role-audience pairs?

Role (you)	Audience
treasurer of the company	president of the company
outside consultant	president of the company
outside consultant	treasurer of the company
staff accountant	president of the company

3. How far should a staff person (like the treasurer) go in making a recommendation to an operational officer (like the president)?

Differences Between Written and Oral Communication

One of the essential differences between oral and written communication is immediacy. As a writer, you face the dilemma of being removed in time and space from your communication partners. Therefore, contextual analysis and audience analysis may be less precise. Writers can shape their message for a given audience, but are less in control over whether the readership is limited to that audience. Even personal letters, intended for a specific and private reading, will often be studied by unintended eyes, as subjects of unauthorized biographies have discovered the hard way. Additionally, writers understand that readers, unlike listeners, cannot contribute to the immediate development and modification of the original message. Feedback is deferred if not discouraged.

Therefore, writing becomes more like a monologue, and historically much more dependent upon the authority (literally, the "authorness") of the writer. (In the organizations where you work, does the staff at any level write as many memos as the supervisors? When the IRS contacts you concerning your tax return, do they phone you or drop by the house?) Readers, in a sense, are dependent upon the directions of writers, at least if they want to remain in the communication relationship. However, readers control the context in that they may choose either to continue or to stop reading.

By contrast, speech is more interactive since any utterance or nonverbal clue potentially invites immediate responses or spontaneous requests for clarification. Even in a formal public speech, most speakers are implicitly available for interruptions and often explicitly structure question-and-answer periods. Although both readers and listeners are participants in communication, listeners become more overt participants.

Practical Considerations

What does all this mean in practical terms? Think about power relationships. Among other things, in most organizational contexts writing a message (a report, a memorandum, a letter, a note) is itself a small expression of power regardless of its content. Writing presumes a degree of organizational permanence and further presumes that the message will be disseminated. It may be associated with other trappings of organizational power, such as access to secretaries and computers. The simple act of writing something asserts that the writer is confident enough to subject the message to response. In one sense, writing pins down the writer to a particular content, but it also pins down the reader to the writer's authority to direct or mandate a basically one-sided situation.

As a writer, therefore, you must be prepared to have your work scrutinized and analyzed, especially by those who might disagree. As the "letters to the editor" pages in newspapers demonstrate, readers are much less tolerant of errors than are conversation partners, and often more incensed at divergent opinions. In contrast, a major principle of conversation is that listeners should try to be cooperative with a speaker's ideas and not "rock the boat" unless absolutely necessary.

On the other hand, speakers might want to anticipate the impermanent nature of talk. While readers can literally *refer* back to what they read yesterday if they want to check on detail, listeners can only *try to recall* what they heard yesterday. They usually do so imperfectly. Some listeners rapidly forget (or never register) both content and context. Listeners, after a time, may dissociate content from context, forgetting, for example, where they heard that the Apex Division is being shut down and all the reasons for its closing.

Face-to-face speech, unless it is captured electronically, trades off permanence for personalization. This is why many managers talk an idea around or send up verbal trial balloons before committing an idea to paper; they want the personalization along with the permanence they'll eventually get with a directive or memo. It's also why effective public speakers like Barbara Bush, Jesse Jackson, or Mario Cuomo build into their speeches memorable phrases, alliteration, and striking metaphors; these memory aids give the message a degree of permanence along with the personalization of seemingly spontaneous speech.

With these differences as backdrop, the next two sections present specific strategies for coping with some of the contextual demands of written and oral communication.

Strategies for Written Communication

Our culture seems to have a reverence for the written word. How many times have you thrown away a book, even if it's an out-of-date accounting text? Most people can't bring themselves to toss old books; they may sell them at a garage sale or donate them to a library, but they don't throw them away. Printed words have a value for us on some unconscious level. When you write for a class or in a professional context, you have to deal with this "set in stone" quality of writing. One way to feel more comfortable with the seeming permanence of your writing is to prepare ahead of time by planning carefully and analyzing context as it relates to writing. Remember to:

1. *Prioritize your objective(s).* Decide on your primary and secondary goals. Are you providing information (secondary goal) in order to persuade (primary goal)? Or, alternatively, are you providing an analysis for a new client (primary goal) in hopes of building a long term business relationship (secondary goal)? Until you are clear on what you hope to accomplish, you are probably not ready to begin sharing your writing. Your choice of words, the organization of your text, even the placement of the words on the page are all affected by the priority of

your objectives. While you might decide to reorder and/or reword these objectives as you write, refer back to your objectives on a regular basis to assure you are staying on track.

2. *Decide what format will best accomplish your objective(s).* Can you best meet your goals through a letter, a brief memo, or a technical report? If you have developed a simple solution for an auditing concern of a client, your most appropriate format may be a brief letter rather than a 75-page detailed report. Your objectives ought to shape your choice of written format. Further, how your writing is packaged can also be a kind of message to readers. Your writing, whatever its internal style or language, can be made more or less formal by such choices as what kind of folder or envelope in which to enclose it, how it is delivered, and whether it includes a personalized handwritten greeting. In addition, decide what content should be presented in paragraph form, what in lists, and what in tables, charts, or graphs.

3. *Analyze the context that has prompted your writing.* Are you responding to a request for information or analysis? Are you initiating the communication? Is your text to serve as a follow-up to a previous communication situation? (If so, have you included enough previous context to remind readers of the broader picture of what is at stake?) Are you working as an employee of an organization (internal role), or are you writing as a consultant (external role)?

4. *Analyze the context in which your text will be read.* Will the text be complete in itself, or is it to be part of an ongoing process? Has your audience requested that you write this text? Will your reader be pleased with what you say, or will your text be a stimulus for conflict? Remember that since you probably won't be present when your text is read, you won't have the opportunity to clear up misunderstandings or smooth ruffled feathers. You need to envision how your text will be received and plan accordingly.

Strategies for Oral Communication

Most of the preceding factors also apply to oral communication—such as prioritizing your objectives, deciding what format will best accomplish your objectives, and analyzing the context. In addition, other factors are primarily important for speakers responsible for presenting specific information and options. Remember that in speaking situations, you will be seen and heard in an immediate context; that is, your audience will evaluate your credibility as a direct part of your message. Who you are, how you conduct yourself, and how you appear to your audience will to a large extent determine their involvement with your ideas. You are part of your message. This fact is crucial, and its importance is impossible to overstate. Therefore, remember to:

1. *Dress appropriately and professionally, taking your cues from the organizational culture and the habits of the people to whom you'll speak.* When in doubt, choose suits and professional wear that are relatively formal; men and women can often remove a jacket to become less formal if the situation warrants.

2. *Make sure ahead of time that you have a clear and realistic idea of how long you're expected to speak to and/or interact with an audience.* This contextual analysis will help you plan the appropriate degree of detail for your talk. Although some people might fear droning on to a bored or restless audience (as then-Governor Bill Clinton did in his 1988 Democratic convention nominating speech for Michael Dukakis), many business speakers also err by being less thorough and detailed than an audience has a right to expect. If an hour is allotted to considering your report, an initial seven-minute presentation might not lay the foundation for subsequent dialogue.

3. *If possible, visit the site of your speech or conference beforehand.* Get the lay of the land. Decide tentatively where you'll sit or stand, and where you'll place any materials to assist you. Arrive early, if appropriate, and be fully prepared before the audience gathers. If you can't visit the site ahead of time, at least find out something about the size of the room and the expected number of people that will be attending.

4. *Remember that you are part of the context for the audience.* Therefore, your mood and even your willingness to smile and chat before the event will set the stage for smoother communication later. Moods and personalities are often subtly infectious. If you look nervous and disinterested, the anxiety level of your communication partners will increase. You may notice your audience's anxiety when you start speaking, and, in a vicious cycle of negativity, you might become concerned as you speak that your audience doesn't like you. It isn't necessarily that they don't like you; more likely, they are mirroring your own attitude.

5. *In your introduction, refer briefly, and preferably in good humor, to any obvious features of context, such as excessive room heat or lateness of the meeting.* Your audience wants to know that you are there with them, physically and psychologically. However, don't dwell on problems, reminding the audience of other things to consider aside from your main purpose for speaking with them. (By the way, lengthy prepared jokes in introductions, unless you're near professional in your skill in adapting them to the immediate audience and context, usually dampen enthusiasm.)

6. *Introduce your purpose and yourself.* The introduction should clarify your perspective (a) relative to the audience, (b) relative to the organi-

zational problem you're attempting to address, and (c) relative to the audience's need to hear what you have to say. Establish credibility succinctly by including whatever personal credentials are relevant, without boasting, and by describing which systematic methods you employed in coming to your conclusions.

7. *Decide if your context and purpose demand precise, exact wording.* If so, you may decide to read some portion of your message directly from a manuscript, as a head of state might do to introduce a news conference. Sometimes, the wording of a statement must be so diplomatically correct in a tense situation that speakers wouldn't trust spontaneous styles of talk. These situations are rare. Most of the time, plan to speak extemporaneously with appropriate visual aids and/or handouts. (See Chapter 6.) **Extemporaneous speaking** means that you are speaking spontaneously, but have prepared your communication plan carefully, and are well aware of the content and context. You have an outline of topics, but are speaking conversationally in adapting them to the immediate situation and audience. You must even be willing to change your outline if an unanticipated question emerges. Extemporaneous speaking differs both from **impromptu speaking** (speaking off the cuff, winging it) and manuscript reading or memorized speaking (which comes across as very formal and inflexible).

These last three items can also support written communication. There might be a specific context problem to mention (e.g., the need to compress a good deal of information into a required two-page limit). As we discuss in later chapters, an introduction sets the stage for what follows. Finally, the same admonition about precise, exact wording applies to written communication as well.

Situation 2: Shaping a Message Based on Role and Audience

You have been asked to explain the concept of *budgeting* and to give some examples.

1. How would the goals, message formats, and contexts of your presentation differ given the following role–audience pairs?

Role (you)	Audience
staff accountant	operating manufacturing managers
staff accountant	hourly workers on production line
staff accountant	secretaries
teacher	high school students
staff accountant	high school students

3. How would your presentation differ in each of the preceding pairs if it were oral instead of written?

Summary

Communication is often taken for granted as basically a message transfer process. In emphasizing the issues of context and purpose, this chapter has taken a different perspective. In order to be an effective communicator, you must realize that readers and listeners are ultimately as much in control of the process as are writers and speakers.

Therefore, this chapter highlighted five general issues. First, communication was defined as the process by which humans interact using messages to structure and make sense of any situation they share in common. Second, we stressed the need for a communication plan, especially in organizations where role differences are clearly defined. Third, we examined the influence of communicator roles on planning organizational messages, whether in writing or speech. Fourth, we compared written and oral communication to see which differences might be critical for communicators to consider. Finally, we surveyed the two modes, written and oral, to emphasize strategies particularly appropriate to each.

Your next step as a communication planner is a more careful consideration of who will be reading or hearing your ideas. Audience analysis is a crucial component of communication success.

How to Approach a Selected Situation

Situation 1: Writing Memos Based on Roles

This situation casts you in different roles writing to different audiences. To start, no matter what the role, the decision of whether to stop the sale of cosmetics should be placed in the context of the overall direction of the company. Thus, in answering the first part of this situation, your decision about what information you would want is affected by the purpose of your analysis. The effect of dropping this part of the business can be looked at from both a strategic perspective as well as a short-term analysis. Not only would you want information relating to the annual lost revenues and costs saved, but also all the interdependencies between selling cosmetics and selling other items. Depending on these relationships, you would want not only quantitative financial information (e.g., labor savings, sale of fixtures, etc.), but also nonfinancial quantitative information (e.g., number of people who buy cosmetics who also buy greeting cards) and qualitative information (e.g., how do customers feel about this decision?).

Each of the role–audience pairs affects how you would present information. The general format of the presentation (a memo) is already defined. Let us compare the difference between being a staff accountant writing the president and an outside consultant writing the president. What does the president expect of a staff accountant as compared to an outside consultant? How can you (in either role) advance your standing not only with the president, but also with the treasurer? What is the organizational culture regarding these different roles?

As a consultant, you would probably have an understanding of the task to be accomplished by your engagement. As a staff member, this might be much more informal in nature. It's an open question about how your role will affect the strength of what you recommend. However, in all the role-audience pairs, you would define the alternatives open to the company, the relevant information to consider, what you recommend, and what you see as the strengths and weaknesses of your recommendation. In developing this general framework, what are the personal involvements of the president, treasurer, or others in this decision? Perhaps the president thinks that you really cannot have a pharmacy without the sale of cosmetics; the president is asking for this information in response to a query from a major stockholder. Knowing this might allow you to couch your recommendation in a way that does not offend either party. This is different than a situation where nobody has any personal feelings and it's just a business question.

3
Analyzing the Audience

Have you ever been in a situation where the speaker is either talking way over your head or seems to be talking down to you? Such situations can leave you feeling frustrated or confused. Clearly your needs were not being addressed. Common sense dictates that all messages should be shaped, at least in part, by the needs of the audience. In this chapter you will consider: (1) the importance of audience analysis for successful communication, (2) the difference between writer-centered and audience-centered texts, (3) questions you can ask when analyzing an audience, and (4) audience analysis strategies for both written and oral communication.

The Role of Audience

Although the need for a communicator to be aware of his or her audience seems almost blatantly obvious, many real-life examples can illustrate how easy it is to misjudge an audience. The defeat of the Equal Rights Amendment (ERA) is a case in point. Since 1982, when all hope of passage disappeared, proponents have tried to analyze what went wrong. One factor in the defeat may have been a failure to carefully analyze a crucial target audience—women. Those who wrote and spoke in favor of the amendment shaped their message to appeal to career women and working mothers. Many women who chose to be stay-at-home mothers or homemakers were disenfranchised by the message. Many felt excluded from the discussion; they often felt ridiculed and defensive about the lifestyle they had chosen. Opponents of ERA took advantage of this miscalculation by emphasizing the lack of concern shown to these women and by evoking suspicions about the motives of the amendment's proponents. These efforts may have reduced the support from many of the at-home women; the lukewarm response from this segment of the audience may have helped defeat the ERA.[1]

---
[1] J. Mansbridge, *Why We Lost the ERA* (Chicago: University of Chicago Press, 1986), pp. 90–112.

Inadequate audience awareness is apparent in many failed and ineffective communication attempts within the business world, as well. You may have had the experience of buying a printer for your computer and being totally frustrated when you tried to set it up, following the directions in the owner's manual. Computer and printer manuals are notoriously difficult for the nontechnical person to use. Most manuals are written on a highly technical level, even though the majority of users are not "computer jocks" and are not conversant with computer jargon.

Just as you may have been frustrated by messages you think are unclear, the people with whom you communicate may also feel a sense of frustration if your words don't fit their experience. Therefore, audience awareness and analysis must be a major component in every communication plan you develop. Your success as a business communicator hinges on your ability to anticipate and meet the needs of an audience. Indeed, the audience must become the focal point of your entire creative/decision-making process. Your audience will affect the format you select, the organizational pattern you use, even the words you choose.

Situation 1: Writing a Memo for Different Audiences

You are employed at a mid-size accounting firm. A few weeks ago, you entered a contest, and you have just been notified that you won first prize (an all-expense-paid trip to Paris). The trip will last two weeks, and fortunately you have enough vacation time to take advantage of this opportunity. You plan to depart one week from today. In the following, consider the choices (tone, word choice, information needs) you would make, given your audience.

1. Write a memo for your friends at the office, telling them of your good fortune.

2. Write a memo to the secretarial support staff of your office, telling them of your plans.

3. Write a letter to one of your clients (Ms. Carole Trask, President of Trask Trucking Company), informing her of your upcoming absence.

Writer-Centered Versus Audience-Centered Texts

To understand why your audience is such a crucial factor in the success or failure of your messages, consider the difference between writer-centered and audience-centered texts. Sometimes as communicators, we need to address only ourselves. Journals, diaries, and classroom or meeting notes are examples of writer-centered texts. No one else will be using this information but you. You can write in shorthand or even hieroglyphics; it doesn't matter, as long as *you* can understand the message. Writer-centered texts do not require any concern for audience; you know what you meant to say, so there is little chance for the message to be misunderstood.

Obviously, only a small portion of your communication as an accountant is writer-centered. Auditors' tick marks are an example. The majority of the time, you are creating and sending messages meant to be audience-centered and interpreted by someone else. Effective communicators never lose track of their audiences; you need to keep your audience foremost in your mind as you plan and execute your message.

Situation 2: Rewriting Writer-Centered Texts

Locate one of your own writer-centered texts from class notes, diaries, or meeting notes. Designate a hypothetical audience for this text (a classmate, a colleague, a professor), and rewrite the information to be audience-centered.

What are the specific changes you needed to make in order to accommodate your intended audience? Note how the appearance of the text changes when you were no longer writing for yourself.

The Process of Audience Analysis

Given the importance of audience and audience-centered communication, you will need to analyze your audience. The following checklist of questions should help you begin the process of audience analysis:

1. Who will be receiving this message?
2. What is my relationship to this audience?
3. What does my audience already know about this subject?
4. What does my audience need to know about this subject?
5. What are my audience's feelings about this subject?
6. What cultural differences might influence how my audience will read or hear messages?

Who Will Be Receiving This Message?

This question is so basic, it may seem completely superfluous. However, often when you anticipate the likely receivers of your message, you may discover an unexpected web of complexity.

Single Audience. You may know for certain that you will have a single reader or listener. Perhaps you are writing a letter detailing new federal tax guidelines to a specific individual, or you are preparing an oral presentation on tax changes for a one-on-one meeting. You can assume that no one else will be reading the letter or attending the meeting. Your job is somewhat easier when you have a single audience; you can make decisions with more certainty because the number of audience factors is limited. Unfortunately, organizational messages are rarely this clear-cut.

Multiple Audience. Sometimes, you will find yourself preparing to address what we will call a multiple audience. The letter you are writing may be addressed to one person, but you will be sending copies to several other people as well. Or your oral presentation may have been requested by one person, but you will be speaking in front of an entire department. Multiple audiences present multiple problems for you as a communicator. The audience may be homogeneous (persons who are similar in age, level of education, and occupation), but more likely, a multiple audience will represent a variety of backgrounds. For multiple audiences you may want to design your message for an average audience member. For example, your oral presentation on tax changes may be attended by people who are familiar with federal tax laws as well as by those who do not have a background in taxation. You can shape your overall report for someone with a mid-range knowledge of taxation. In order to include those who are less knowledgeable, you can stop and say, "I realize this information may be new to some of you. I will try to include the definitions you need. Let me know if you have questions or if I'm going too fast." To acknowledge the more advanced awareness of some audience members, you can say, "Many of you are familiar with these procedures, but I felt a brief summary would focus the issues for all of us."

Unknown Audience. Often, you will be in the position of communicating with an unknown or unspecifiable audience, one you can't precisely anticipate even with a demographic analysis. You are preparing a company-wide memo, but you are uncertain as to exactly who will actually read it; you are writing a magazine article on auditing software; or you are preparing a speech for a national accounting convention. In each of these situations you cannot be certain of the characteristics of your audience. You will have to make a choice whether to aim for the middle ground (perhaps acknowledging this fact early in the text, but making every effort to include individuals on both sides of the middle) or whether to address those closer to, say, the higher end of the spectrum of what the audience could know. For some writing contexts, you have the option of adding an appendix or list of references for those who need additional background information and/or for those who want to learn more about your subject.

Target Audience. Many speakers and writers know their ideas will be received by some people in the audience who ultimately have no influence on how their overall message will be used. For example, a speech that irritates or even alienates most listeners, but which impresses the comptroller (your target audience) can still be considered successful. Thus, determine who your target audience is. This might be your entire audience or some specified subset.

What Is My Relationship to This Audience?

Your relationship to the audience requires analysis of the communication context, as discussed in Chapter 2. First consider your position relative to your intended audience. You might be writing to a peer or a colleague; a professor or your supervisor; a younger classmate or a subordinate. Most of us find ourselves functioning within several relational hierarchies every day. Within an organization you may be part of a team of auditors; you may have a manager who oversees your work; and you may have an assistant whose work you supervise. Obviously your interaction with these various individuals will be affected and shaped by your relationship to them. These relationships will affect tone (formal or informal) as well as word choice.

In addition to thinking in terms of a hierarchical relationship, you also need to consider the qualities that characterize your relationship to your audience. You could be friends, adversaries, or strangers. The audience might be clients or persons you are hoping to do business with in the future. For example, you will probably have established credibility with current clients; they know you and you have an ongoing relationship. Prospective clients, on the other hand, do not know you. Thus, with the latter audience, you might need to be more formal and to say things in a way that helps to establish you as a credible source. You might state, "the problems you pose seem quite similar to ones we helped address for the XYZ Company." Thus, relationships will be important criteria as you make writing and editing decisions.

What Does My Audience Already Know About This Subject?

Answering this question will help you decide how much background information you need to include or how technical your language and approach can be. If you are dealing with an audience that shares your level of knowledge and expertise, then you do not need to elaborate on the information you share or define terms often used. When writers or speakers spend time telling the audience things they already know, they risk boring or even insulting their readers or listeners. Readers don't want to be condescended to, nor do they want to waste their time wading through a text full of information they already have. If you are an outside consultant and your audience is members of management of the firm that hired you, you wouldn't want to begin your analysis with a long history of the company. You assume readers are already aware of the company's past; don't make the readers skim through extraneous paragraphs in hopes of getting to the vital information they need.

In speaking you can rapidly adjust to your audience's level of understanding. You might come prepared to explain the qualities of two different machines only to find your audience is already familiar with them and does not need that information. Speakers should be flexible enough to adjust to such situations.

Overestimating the level of knowledge and expertise of your audience is all too common, as readers of computer manuals will attest. Your message will not be understood if you talk over the heads of your audience or use **jargon** (specialized terminology that only experts in a given field are likely to know) that they do not understand. Imagine you are working for a client who owns a small business, but who has little knowledge of cost accounting techniques. This client wants predictions about possible profits for the coming year; however, if you send a letter that includes unexplained terms such as "contribution margin" or "cost-volume-profit analysis," the information will be of little value to your client. If you need to include such terminology, then you will want to define and explain any and all terms that may be foreign to your audience.

Remember that effective definitions are succinct, accurate, and relate the defined term directly to what the audience *already* understands. Thus, concrete examples are more helpful than textbook precision. For example: "'Overhead' refers to business expenses that are not directly included in the merchandise we sell—such as the rent we pay on those fancy new copy machines."

Anticipating the average level of audience knowledge accurately will save your audience from being bored or being insulted. During an oral presentation, you should be aware of when it will be necessary to cut back on what you had planned to present or when to fill in the blanks in order to bring your audience up to speed. In Chapters 6 and 8 we discuss how to find out more of what your audience already knows.

Situation 3: Creating Messages for Different Audiences

Consider the following: "Product costs involve inventoriable costs as compared to period costs which are expensed in the period incurred. Besides direct and indirect variable costs, common manufacturing overhead is applied to each unit of product using appropriate drivers."

Rewrite this message for each of the following audiences, attending separate educational seminars on manufacturing accounting.

1. A group of production managers.
2. A group of sales managers.
3. A group of union officers who represent hourly production workers.
4. High school students.

What Does My Audience Need to Know About This Subject?

This question builds on answers to the previous question. Suppose you are preparing an oral presentation for a client in response to an auditing procedures review. Your goal is to persuade this company to adopt better procedures for handling cash. After assessing your audience, you feel that as a group they are unfamiliar with the procedures you are going to suggest; therefore, in order to persuade them to accept your suggestions, you will have to spend some time during the presentation explaining the basics of the method as well as providing reasons why this method is the best choice given their circumstances. You should plan to fill the gap between what is known and what is needed. However, you should go only as far as needed and not beyond. For example, explain only relevant procedures, not all potential controls.

What Are My Audience's Feelings About This Subject?

Suppose you need to write a letter reprimanding a staff member or a critique of a group presentation made in your tax class. These communication situations are sensitive because your message could trigger emotional responses in your audience. While writing a reprimand, remember that few people enjoy being criticized. The usual reaction is defensiveness. If your goal is to provide constructive criticism with the hope that the individual will learn from his or her mistakes, you first have to break through the resistance that usually develops when someone feels attacked. Taking into account how your reader is going to feel about this letter will help you to create a text that acknowledges those feelings, but focuses on the opportunity for improvement. Critiquing a group project involves many of the same issues. You want to point out weaknesses you noted, but you don't want to alienate your classmates. By realizing how your audience may be affected by your words, you can make better decisions as a communicator.

Since emotions often filter or deflect the intended message, writers and speakers should put themselves into the position of the audience and try to take the reader's or listener's perspective. Imagine opening and reading that letter of reprimand. Imagine receiving a critique of your group project—not as *you* personally would read it, but instead as the critiqued persons, with *their* feelings, goals, and jobs in mind. When you try to consider communication from your audience's point of view, you can better anticipate emotional problem areas and plan your message accordingly. Remember that in this imaginative identification, which some therapists and social scientists have called empathy, your *own* biases are still at work. Thus, just because *you* would rather be complimented constantly throughout the day, don't assume that others have the same preference. Although it sounds nice, "Do unto others as you would have them do unto you," may at times be poor advice for communicators if the "others" don't like the same kinds of "doing unto."

The examples so far highlight situations where it seems obvious that feelings would be affected. There are many situations where it's not so obvious, but feelings are just as important. For example, if you are analyzing which of several mutually exclusive projects to recommend to operating management, remember that each project might have its own champion in upper management and/or might have been a pet project of a lower-level manager. You cannot ignore the interaction of what you say and how you say it in relation to feelings. The buy-lease decision on pages 25 and 26 in Chapter 2 illustrates this point.

Situation 4: Shaping Communication for Specific Audiences

The Athics Company purchased a machine a year ago for $500,000. Originally, the company decided to depreciate the asset over 8 years using the straight-line method. The Chief Financial Officer of the company has been discussing changing the depreciation to a 12-year life. He is concerned about current earnings and sees this as a way to lower expenses with no harm to the company. You are concerned about this change since you believe that the useful life of the asset is unaffected and that this proposed change would be unethical. Write brief memoranda using the following pairs of roles and audiences. What are the differences in what you said and how you said it given your role and the audience?

Role (You)	Audience
Assistant to Chief Financial Officer	Chief Financial Officer
Staff member of firm that audits Athics	Your superior
Staff member of firm that audits Athics	Chief Financial Officer
Partner of firm that audits Athics	Chief Financial Officer
Vice President-Operations of Athics	Chief Financial Officer

What Cultural Differences Might Influence How My Audience Will Read or Hear Messages?

In this era of growing international trade, you could easily find yourself dealing with executives from other countries who have alternative ways of communicating within their cultures. You will be communicating using the same language (perhaps English), but you need to be aware of possible problems that can occur with nonnative speakers of English. Many phrases Americans use are often misunderstood by people for whom English is not their first language. These phrases, called idioms, do not mean exactly what their words imply. Examples of idioms in American English include: "kick the bucket," "deep six the report," and "a Catch-22 situation." If you know your audience will include nonnative English speakers, you will need to plan your communication carefully and avoid using words and phrases that could confuse listeners or readers.

Cultural differences are not limited to international communication. Many cultures, including ethnic and religious groups, coexist within the United States. Most people are sensitive to their own cultural group, but they often forget their group is just one part of a multicultural society. As a professional, you need to be aware of and sensitive to cultural diversity. For example, it is common in some Eastern and Asian-American cultures for people to act as if they are agreeing with something even when they are unsure or really disagree; it's a matter of manners. Think also of recent controversies about sports teams: the Washington Redskins and the Atlanta Braves (with signs saying "Scalp the . . . ." hanging in the stadium). Using wording or examples that would alienate cultures such as Native Americans also runs the risk of alienating others in the audience who are sensitive to cultural diversity.

Audience Analysis Strategies for Written Communication

Writers have a major disadvantage when it comes to their audiences. Most writing is not read in the presence of the author. This naturally results in a lack of immediacy; as a writer, you will not be able to assess your readers' reactions as they read. You will not be there to answer questions, nor can you use body language and voice inflection to clarify your message. Readers can work only with the text in front of them, and your readers cannot read your mind. The message you write has to be clear the first time; your message is represented only by the words on the page. No other factors can come into play. This does not ignore your ability to edit and rewrite something until you're satisfied with it. However, once a written message is delivered the preceding points apply.

This lack of immediate feedback challenges writers to create accessible texts that lead readers through ideas clearly and logically. Once you have analyzed your reader's needs through the use of the six questions discussed earlier, you also need to be aware of the importance of the surface conventions that are vital for communicating effectively. These surface conventions include paragraphing, spelling, and punctuation. Even the most careful audience analysis will be of little use if you create ambiguous sentences or if you fail to order your information into logical paragraphs. The reader needs to know where one sentence stops and another begins, where one idea stops and a new one begins, and how your thoughts are related to one another. A more complete discussion of surface conventions is included in Chapter 6.

Here then are strategies you can use for written communication, which reinforce the general principles of audience analysis:

1. Determine as nearly as possible who your target audience is.
2. Use the audience analysis questions listed earlier in this chapter.
3. Keep a mental picture of your audience as you begin to write. Throughout the writing process imagine that you are having a conversation with your readers.
4. Decide on the best possible written format for your audience. Will your readers respond best to a formal letter, memorandum, or report? Can your message be given informally? Does your audience need extensive supporting materials (graphs, spreadsheets, etc.)?
5. Determine what tone you wish to establish in your text. Do you want to be friendly and conversational? Do you need to remain more distanced from your readers through the use of more formal language? Tone is established through word choice, and once you have decided on the tone you want your writing to have, you need to maintain that tone throughout the text.
6. Decide on the style of writing that best suits your audience. Again, you can choose between informal and formal styles. An informal style can include using contractions and a more conversational approach. A formal style would be less personal and follow the conventions of business writing. Perhaps your audience would respond best to a concise technical writing style that economizes on words.

Audience Analysis Strategies for Oral Communication

Remember that *immediacy* is the basic feature distinguishing face-to-face speech from written communication. Although most basic audience analysis strategies apply equally well when writing or speaking to audiences, conversational or public speakers must account for this added subtlety. Unfortunately, most speakers ignore the potential for audience analysis in the immediate experience of speaking.

Think about which audience analysis factors are most relevant to the spontaneity of a particular public speaking situation or an interpersonal conversation. Consider what you can do to maximize your effectiveness on the spot. The following are some useful strategies:

1. Recall what you know (if anything) about audience members' previous habits in other speaking situations. You may be able to infer what kinds of reactions are more likely when you speak.
2. Develop contingency plans based on different possible reactions from the audience. Don't rely on the audience or any of its members to react in a particular way for which you've planned. In prac-

tical terms, this could mean, among other things, that: your funniest story may be met with blanketing silence; your question-and-answer period may stimulate zero questions; your impassioned call for a volunteer may be futile. A more positive aspect of this suggestion is that speakers who know ahead of time that they will be speaking to an enthusiastic and responsive group need to anticipate how they will control the time or put the discussion on track if the audience enjoys the ideas and begins to run with them.

3. Monitor the listeners' nonverbal responses while you speak to obtain cues for adjusting the remaining parts of your message. This advice is easier to assert than to practice, and even a detailed summary of the "hows" of such nonverbal sensitivity is beyond this book. Entire books are devoted to analyzing nonverbal behavior as cues to human emotion; however, what follows are some useful, if overgeneralized, indicators.

- Eye contact in general North American culture usually signals the attention (though not always the interest) of the listener. Eye contact is less reliable as an indicator of attention among some other cultural groups because for many people averting the eyes is a sign of respect.

- Posture and movement can be reasonable indicators of audience attention. Generally, interested listeners tend to exhibit a forward-leaning posture facing the speaker, and do not fidget.

- Facial expressions, though often ambiguous, can be helpful to monitor. Look for slightly different things than you might think, though. Instead of simply noting whether people are smiling or frowning as positive or negative feedback, be aware of when they smile or frown. Bored listeners can paint smiles on their faces as facades, and fascinated listeners can frown as they struggle internally with a challenging idea that intrigues them. What you want to check is whether the smiles correspond to the humorous sections of the talk, and whether the frowns might be a generalized negative reaction. Remember, too, that few audience members are totally in control of the appearance of their own nonverbal cues and may disclose their emotions in quite varied ways.

- Silence can have positive as well as negative dimensions. Silence in response to your requests for involvement or interaction may mean that your audience couldn't care less, or it may mean that listeners care so much about your message that they want to give it some serious thought. Serious thought takes time. Don't automatically assume your audience is alienated if they're silent.

You may protest that all this on-the-scene analysis is hard. You could ask questions such as: Isn't it likely to take my mind off my own thoughts? Won't I lose my place? Won't I forget where I'm going with my ideas? The answer to these good questions is simple, but hard to swallow for a speaker who's not willing to practice. Yes, immediate audience analysis will deflect you from the development of your own thoughts if you're inadequately prepared or if you aren't self-confident in the first place. Speaking with a group, or conversing with another person, for that matter, is very much like improvisational jazz. It doesn't make sense for a saxophonist to say to a pianist, "I wish you wouldn't play while I'm trying to create my own music; it distracts me." The basis of improvisation is playing off the ideas of others. Without that sensitivity, that flexibility, it's not jazz. To extend the analogy to communication, there are no solo acts involved in speaking to a group. Everything is ensemble work. Without the flexibility of audience awareness, it's not effective communication. The success of the communication is the success of the speaker and listener(s) creating meaning together. As a speaker, you must practice not only how to prepare and express ideas, but also how to listen and monitor how those ideas are growing or deteriorating among your "musical" partners.

Situation 5: Developing Oral Presentations for Specific Audiences

You are the new Chief Financial Officer of a company that has just been bought from its parent. The Board of Directors of the new company consists of hourly employees of the company, members of management, and some outside investors. You have been reading some literature saying that it's important for everyone from the board down to hourly employees to know how to read financial statements.

1. If you were making a presentation to the Board of Directors instructing them how to read financial statements,
    a. Would you want to do it in writing or orally?
    b. What would be an appropriate approach (plan) for such a presentation?
    c. What visual aids would you want to employ?
2. If you were making a presentation to hourly workers in the factory instructing them how to read financial statements,
    a. Would you want to do it in writing or orally?
    b. What would be an appropriate approach (plan) for such a presentation?
    c. What visual aids would you want to employ?

Summary

Audience awareness is perhaps the most crucial factor in the success or failure of any communication plan. Effective communicators never forget their audiences, and they use their audience's needs as the major component in all the decisions they make as they plan for communication. The people you interact with expect and deserve accessible and comprehensible messages.

How to Approach a Selected Situation

Situation 3: Creating Messages for Different Audiences

In each case, the audience is not familiar with the technical jargon included in the original message. You will want to form your response taking into consideration the frame of reference (knowledge, experiences) of your target audience. Here are some suggestions.

Production Managers. In order to comply with accounting rules, we divide costs into two pools: costs associated with everything you and your people do in the plant and costs associated with the front office and sales department. When we look at the cost of any particular product, say Model 43093, we look at the cost of materials and components (like the housing) we buy and the costs of the hourly labor for making the product. In addition, as you all know, there are a lot of costs out there that are not just in materials and labor. For example, John's department maintains all the equipment and Sally's does all our in-plant engineering. We look at how those costs are associated with each product and give each product a share not only of these specific costs, but also of general costs like heat, light, building insurance, and so on. All of these supporting costs are called overhead. Thus, when we build 100 units of Model 43093, we take the costs associated with these 100 units (materials/components, labor, factory overhead) and associate those costs with those units. Let's say the total is $30 per unit. If 100 units are in inventory, then they are valued at $3,000. Later, if 50 are sold, inventory is lowered to $1,500 while $1,500 appears in the income statement as the cost associated with sales of 50 units. Let's compare this to sales costs; these costs are part of the monthly cost of doing business and appear in the monthly income statement. These costs are not related to whether a product is kept in inventory or sold.

Sales Managers. In order for you to know more about how we set prices, let's talk about how we divide our costs for financial accounting. All costs are either associated with what we do in the plant or what we do in the front office or in sales. Your salaries and other costs are expenses each month; we lower income given these expenses. In contrast, costs associated with making our products only affect income when a unit is sold. As you know from talking to the estimators in the plant, basically our product costs are the materials and components we buy, the labor we use to make and assemble the products, and the general plant costs, called overhead, that we assign to each product.

Union Officers. I know you are all interested in how we look at costs here in the plant. Part of how we do things is related to what we have to do to create financial statements for the banks, our owners, and the IRS. Rules call for us dividing our costs to those in the plant and those in the front office and sales. Let's look at plant costs. For example, how about Model 43093 which is made in part in several departments. We take all the material and components (like the housing) we buy and add on the costs of the union hourly workers. You know that your people record the hours they work on each job. This is part of how we can see what a job costs. We also add the costs associated with about everything else in the plant. Thus, we take some of Joe's time in Quality Control, Pete's in managing the racks where we store materials, and Sarah's for moving stuff with the forklift and add that to the cost for every product. In addition, some general costs like heat, light, supervision, etc. are added. All these supporting costs are called overhead. When we're all done, we have the cost of each product consisting of its materials/components, labor, and share of overhead. When we make 100 Model 4309's, we can then value them at that cost whether we keep them in inventory or sell them.

Here is where the big difference comes in with the plant costs and the other costs. For our income statement, we show only plant costs associated with the products we sell. However, for the front office and sales costs, everything we spend each month is shown as an expense for that month.

High School Students. As accountants, we are governed by rules on how to deal with information. One of these rules requires that we divide costs into two parts: costs associated with making our products and other costs (like the general management of the company and sales). You are all familiar with textbooks, so let's use them as an example. If we were a company printing and binding texts, we would keep track of the costs of the paper, ink, cover material, glue (all generally called materials), the labor associated with the people on the presses and binding machines, and all of the other plant costs. Taken together, we can come up with a cost per book. The difficult part is assigning general costs (like the cost of supervisors, engineering, heat, light, and plant insurance—collectively called overhead) to each book. Some of these items are easier to associate with the book (like maintenance of the machines on which it is printed) while some are almost impossible to trace (like light or the plant manager's salary). However, we find a way to assign all these costs. Thus, whatever books are in the plant are valued at a cost consisting of materials, labor, and overhead. When the company sells books, those costs are shown as an expense. Thus, the company would show revenue for the sales less the costs of the books sold. In addition, the company would also deduct costs associated with the general running of the business (administrative and sales costs).

As you read the preceding, you can see that parts of each might be used for the others. These are just samples of what you could do. How do your statements compare? Where do you believe yours are better? Not as good? Why?

4
Determining Content and Approach

You have been asked to analyze the possible purchase of a large piece of equipment costing $6,000,000. Your report will go to the Vice President of Operations and she will then generate a recommendation to the President. There are several ways to approach this task. You could start with the marketing people to get information about customer needs and projected sales to utilize the equipment. Another approach would be to start with operating plant personnel and the engineers and begin estimating operating characteristics and costs. There are other ways to start—each with its own advantages and disadvantages, each possibly leading down different paths toward your final analysis.

In fact, you might find that an approach or part of your analysis leads to a partial redefinition of the task. While you are interested in whether to buy the equipment, you might find some interesting aspects of the competitive environment that you want to include, even though they go beyond your original purpose.

This example illustrates an important aspect of communication planning: content and approach, the final ingredients of any communication plan. You will consider: (1) the types of approaches you can use for conveying your information, (2) possible organizational schemes and formats, (3) the process of incorporating information from other sources into your own message (synthesis), (4) sources for researching your topic, and (5) choice of graphics to support your information. In this chapter we do not separate strategies for written communication from those for oral contexts, since the same questions serve to guide your content decisions as both a writer and a speaker.

Content as Part of a Communication Plan

In previous chapters we looked at two vital parts of a communication plan: purpose and audience. Knowing your intended outcome and being aware of your intended audience are essential before you can begin to create and shape your message. However, before you begin to draft a letter, report, or presentation, you need to make some decisions about the content of your message and how best to focus what you have to say. During this stage of planning, you first need to determine what you might want to include in your message. Do you have the information you need or should you do some additional research? What is the best organizational scheme to use? Is your information best represented visually, and if so, what sort of graphic presentation will work best? All of these aspects need to be considered as you prepare to put pen to paper or words on screen.

Thinking through this part of your communication plan may take only a few minutes while you jot down some notes and reminders to yourself, or it may involve several weeks of gathering and preparing data. Determining content and approach are just as important as understanding purpose and analyzing audience in the overall success of your communication. Thus, you will want to approach every communication situation with a clear sense of purpose, audience, and content (*a communication plan*) before beginning the process of drafting.

Deciding on an Approach

Choosing an approach is much like a manufacturer choosing a package for a particular product. In many cases, the way the product is packaged will influence the way the public perceives the product and may affect its overall acceptance. The same is true for communication. The way you decide to *package* your information will greatly influence the outcome of your message. Although packaging a message includes details such as paper quality or letterhead design, we are going to concentrate on the kinds of rhetorical approaches you can take in presenting your message. These approaches are not mutually exclusive; rather, you will make choices that combine elements of all of them.

Analysis Versus Description

Many people have a difficult time distinguishing between description and analysis as approaches to communication. Although some communication contexts may require that you provide descriptive information, most of the communication situations accountants (both students and professionals) encounter involve analyzing information.

The difference between description and analysis is the difference between recapping and probing. It's the difference between writing a pure statement of facts and writing an investigative report. When you are using a descriptive approach to communication, you are simply giving a recap of the data; perhaps you are summarizing last month's financial results. However, analysis necessitates that you probe into the information. This probing is accomplished by answering the questions,

"So what?" or "What are the ramifications of this information?" When you provide answers to these types of probing questions, you have entered the realm of analysis. In terms of the previous example, a mere description may not satisfy your readers or listeners. By shifting to address the reasons why last month's results did or did not meet expectations, you are providing an analysis of the situation.

For example, suppose a company's accounting system yields the following information:

	Budget	Actual
Sales	$1,000,000	$900,600
Units	100,000	94,800
Price	$10/unit	$9.50/unit

A *description* would be:

> The budget called for 100,000 units to be sold at $10 each or total revenues of $1,000,000. Actual sales were $900,600 with 94,800 units sold at an average of $9.50 per unit.

Analysis could include:

> Sales fell short from expectations both in price and quantity ($9.50 vs. $10.00 per unit; 94,800 vs. 100,000 units). This was caused by a price war in the industry. Our volume went down before we could react in the marketplace by lowering our own prices. Thus, both volume and average price suffered. When we are faced with this kind of competitive pressure in the future, we will have to take more immediate action.

Many complex texts (reports, proposals, or case studies) will require that you use both description and analysis. Without both, the audience is left hanging and will no doubt come to its own conclusions about the information you have presented as well as its own conclusions about the quality of your thought and effort.

Formal Versus Informal Approach

Not all the writing or speaking you will do needs to be as formal as an article in *The Accounting Review* or *Harvard Business Review*. Deciding the level of formality of your approach involves a choice between formal or informal language which will determine the overall tone of the text. Tone can be suggested in both written and spoken language. In written language, tone refers to the overall feeling evoked by the words; while in oral language, tone is further demonstrated by the ways the words are spoken; pitch, rate, volume of inflection all contribute to perceived formality. A formal tone is created by using words and sentences that create a distance from the reader. Formal language avoids contractions and usually does not address the reader directly. It may rely more on *passive voice* ("It was determined that . . .") than *active* ("The comp-

Situation 1: Recognizing Analysis and Description

Workers Using Data-Processing Equipment

1950

1960

1970

1980

Each symbol represents one million workers

Required:

1. Write three facts illustrated by this pictograph. (Description)
2. Name three groups that might have an interest in this data.
3. Write a brief analysis of the data for each of the three groups you listed in Step 2.

Source: Michael H. Markel, *Technical Writing: Situations and Strategies*, 2d Ed. (New York: St. Martin's Press, Inc., 1988), 258.

---

troller discovered . . ."), although formal language can also include the active voice. This is the language of an accounting standard or of audit reports. Informal language is more like the language of everyday conversation. Although it will not usually include slang, an informal approach will be more natural-sounding, will use contractions, and will address the reader directly. We have generally tried to write this book from this perspective.

Remember your audience analysis when making formality decisions. As a communicator, you will need to decide whether your message is best related to your particular audience through formal or informal language. Your decision about formality will also be influenced by the communication context. Some organizational cultures and situations demand formality while others do not.

Situation 2: Choosing Between Formal and Informal Approaches

In which of the following situations would you choose to use a formal approach and which informal? Clearly state why you have made your choices.

1. You are the speaker at the local meeting of the Association of Government Accountants. You are giving a presentation regarding new software available in the field.

2. You are the local Plant Manager of a multinational firm. The Board of Directors is having their meeting at your plant this month. You have been asked to make a presentation regarding your plant's operations.

3. You have been asked to be a professional witness in a utility regulation case. You are to write a brief dealing with the relevant issues of the case.

4. You are writing a report about regional operations that will be included in a more general report going to stock analysts interested in your company.

Direct Versus Indirect Approach

A final type of approach you should consider involves the degree of directness you wish to employ. This issue is most important when you are dealing with sensitive areas where people might have feelings about what you are going to say. Reports that include criticism, any sense of bad news, or that involve pet projects, pet peeves, or favorite topics of some readers or listeners are examples of where your choice to be direct or indirect might be crucial.

Once you find yourself in such a situation, you have the choice of being direct with your communication or approaching the message in a more roundabout (indirect) way. There are sound reasons for using either approach. At times your decision will be influenced by the nature of your audience; other times you will choose between direct and indirect based on your comfort with one of these approaches. However, even if you are more comfortable with one approach or the other, you must be aware when each is appropriate.

The difference between the two approaches is apparent in the synonyms used for each. Direct is also blunt, candid, specific, frank, and plain; indirect is circuitous, oblique, roundabout, and vague. When you are direct, the audience immediately knows exactly what you are thinking and why you are thinking it. In an indirect approach, the audience has to infer more from what you are saying. Consider the following examples of direct and indirect approaches.

Direct: The Vice President of Finance seems more interested in building his power base than in providing useful information to operating managers.

Indirect: Smooth operations depend on the Vice President of Finance's office providing useful information to the operating managers.

In the first example, there is a direct criticism of the vice president. This might be appropriate in a case analysis where you are a student writing to a teacher—there are no egos to hurt in that situation. If you were writing a report evaluating performance given certain criteria, you might choose the direct approach and then support your evaluation with reasoning and evidence. For a report dealing with general operations, especially one that will be read by many people, the indirect approach would seem better. Note that the preceding illustration of the direct approach is strongly stated. You can be as direct in many other ways.

As you can see from this example, the indirect approach often leaves out particular information. In this case, having direct criticism of the vice president might not be useful. One side effect of saying things indirectly, though, is leaving your readers or listeners to wonder if there is some hidden meaning in what you are saying. Thus, they might come to a wrong conclusion about any subtext.

Situation 3: Creating an Indirect and a Direct Text

You have been part of a team assessing the effectiveness and efficiency of the Vice President of Finance's office. His duties include not only generation of external reports to shareholders and taxing authorities, but also the coordination of information for management decision making. Your team has concluded that the vice president has not been doing a good job in providing managerial information while he has been doing an adequate job in his other responsibilities. In addition, you have sufficient evidence to conclude that he wants to have as much personal power within the organization as possible. He wants to be seen as indispensable and the confidant of the president.

Required: Using the guidelines and the illustrations for direct and indirect methods, write two to three sentences using each of these two approaches. Do not use the same content or wording as the example in the text.

Many of us choose to use a direct or indirect approach based on the way we like to receive sensitive news. This can have its good and bad points. While it's important to think about how you would feel if you received information using the direct or indirect approach, it is also important not to let your own biases influence what is appropriate in a situation and to think about the audience and how the audience would feel. What is your intended purpose and who is your audience? These are important questions to answer before making a choice.

In deciding on an approach for either oral or written communication, you have to determine whether your task calls for description and/or analysis. In addition, depending on your role, audience, and the task and context, you will choose to present in a formal or informal and direct or indirect manner. These choices are all part of your communication plan.

Chapter 7 deals with some specific formats (e.g., reports, letters, memoranda). However, let's look at a couple of these in light of this discussion. If you were writing a letter to a client regarding the application of an accounting rule, odds are that this would be fairly formal, direct, and would include both a description of the problem and your analysis of suggested solutions. Compare this to an internal memorandum dealing with a sensitive subject. If this memo is addressed to your subordinate, you might be fairly informal, describe the problem at hand, and might choose to be indirect depending on the sensitivity of the issue.

These same concerns and choices apply to oral communication as well. A report to the Board of Directors on next year's plans might be formal, direct, and both descriptive and analytical. If you were giving instructions regarding the content of a training seminar, you might be informal, direct, and mostly descriptive. As you can see, the combination of choices you make really is specific to the situation at hand, whether you are dealing with an oral or written context.

Choosing an Organizational Scheme

Once you have thought through your combination of choices in terms of approach, you are ready to think about how best to organize your information for a clear presentation.

The Three S's

A primary organization scheme is one that can be used in almost every communication context from short memos to long speeches. It involves dividing your presentation or text into three steps or segments:

Say It

Support It

Say It Again

When you use this pattern, you use the opening section (introduction) to present your most important point(s); you use your middle sections (body) to support or illustrate your ideas; and you finish your communication (conclusion) by restating your main point(s). Practically speaking, this format introduces important ideas up front and closes by reaffirming those same main points. Of course, the "say it again" advice does not mean to present the ideas verbatim. A repetition of the introduction as part of your conclusion will insult readers and listeners. Think of introductions and conclusions together as the frame around the picture of your text. They should complement one another as well as clearly structure the overall message for your audience. While the three S's are important in both written and oral communication, they are especially useful in longer oral settings since listeners are unable to go back to a previous page the way readers can.

Topical Organization

Organizing ideas by subjects or topics is common, and clear to most readers or listeners who are familiar with the terminology you use to identify the topics. In preparing a report dealing with your firm's new corporate headquarters in Detroit, you may wish to present the implications of the move in four parts: (1) changeover costs, (2) cost of living differences, (3) availability of materials, and (4) corporate image. If discussing the adoption of a new FASB rule, topics could include (1) related rules, (2) points of view raised by public accounting firms and/or major corporations, and (3) projected impact, for example. Take care not to divide your organization into too many subsections; three or four divisions should be appropriate for most topically organized messages.

Chronological Order

When you order your information chronologically, you are presenting the information in relation to time. You take your reader forward through time; you detail events from first to last. This organizational pattern works best when you are tracing the history of a problem or are recounting the steps in a process. This pattern is one of the easiest for a communicator to use because the events or steps have already ordered themselves. The writer or speaker does not have to make decisions about where to start or how to place information sequentially. Using a chronological order is appropriate if you are recapping the history of how you have come to a particular decision to purchase a new division or when dealing with tax cases that are precedents for an issue you are researching. If addressing the adoption of an FASB rule, the time frame of the process is the focus, and a chronological order is how you want to organize your discussion and analysis. Be especially careful about using this technique. Because it is the easiest to write, it is often used inappropriately. Think about the audience. If they do not care about the chronology, this is not a good approach.

Cause-Effect or Effect-Cause

In this ordering system you can begin with a cause and explain the effect or begin with a discussion of an effect followed by an explanation of the cause. Either way, you are helping your readers to see the relationship between the two. Assume you are dealing with interest rates for loans and how they are influenced by the general rate of inflation in the economy. With cause-effect you could say:

> Since the general rate of inflation has remained fairly low over the last few years and is not expected to rise significantly, most lenders are not building an inflation adjustment into the rate of interest they are going to charge.

On the other hand, the effect-cause relationship could be described as:

> Interest rates are going to be fairly constant over the next few years. This is especially true since inflation has remained fairly low and is not expected to rise significantly.

Again, looking at the adoption of an accounting rule by the FASB, usually some question has arisen (cause) that led to the discussion and adoption of the new rule (effect).

Decreasing Order of Importance

This pattern for organization will work when you have several different points to make, but some of them are more important than others. In this pattern you will lead with your most important point and then follow with the rest of your less important ideas. As a communicator, you may want to choose this pattern if there is any chance your reader is not going to read your entire text or if you are concerned that you might not keep your audience's full attention over a long oral presentation. By beginning with your most important point, you can be fairly sure that your audience will grasp it.

Increasing Order of Importance

This pattern of organization is the opposite of the preceding one. Here you are using your less important details to build a foundation for the most important point which you will deliver last. This pattern often is the choice for persuasive contexts. Assume that you want to convince your audience that the alternative you have chosen is the best one. You can begin by listing the five options that you considered. Then you can show why you rejected four of them in the order of the weakest to the strongest of that group. Finally, you would show why you adopted your recommendation and how it answers the criticisms you had of the other four. The psychology of this approach is that your audience will remember the last thing read or the last thing heard. You can see why building a strong foundation and ending with a strong argument is often a good idea. This brings us to two additional topics to include in your organizational scheme: summary and synthesis.

Summary and Synthesis

Besides deciding on an approach and choosing an organizational scheme, there are smaller refinements to consider, including summarizing your analysis and synthesizing outside information.

Preparing a Summary

In some contexts you will need to summarize information for your audience. In long reports, this might take the form of an overview called an **executive summary**, a topic covered in Chapter 7. However, even in shorter reports, it is often important to have a brief summary at the beginning and/or at the end of a presentation as a means to focus or refocus attention on important matters.

The easiest way to understand a summary is to think of its uses in other more familiar contexts: a synopsis of a piece of literature (Cliffs Notes) or a sports highlights film. Each of these examples provides an overview of the subject being presented. A synopsis of a book excerpts only those details that someone who has not read the book will need to know in order to have a sense of the entire text. Likewise, a sports highlights film does not include every play in a game, only the important scoring plays or turning points in the competition. After reading the synopsis of a book or watching a sports highlights film, the audience will feel as though they generally understand the book or the flow of the game. By providing a summary, you supply enough information that others will be able to understand the situation without actually having been part of the proceedings.

As mentioned, many reports begin with an executive summary that provides all the relevant information from the report. If written properly, the executive summary should stand alone; the reader can then choose whether or not to read the entire report. In fact, time savings is one of the main reasons for creating executive summaries: people who are too busy to read the entire document can obtain crucial information at a glance.

Once you understand that a summary is an overview of the entire context, you can create a summary by noting all the vital details and giving a capsulized version of their content. Remember that any summary does more than merely introduce a topic; a summary serves as a complete rundown of all the pertinent information.

CHAPTER FOUR 63

Situation 4: Summarizing

Pick up a recent copy of *The Wall Street Journal*. Read all three main articles that start on the front page. Choose one of these articles.

Required:

1. You are the newsletter editor of a publication that summarizes important articles from the financial press. Write a summary of the article you chose to be included in the newsletter. The summary is to convey the full scope of the article. Limit your summary to 150 words. You will also need a headline not to exceed one line. Give your summary to another person who has not read the article. Ask that person to tell you the gist of the article after reading your 150-word summary.

2. You are the news anchor on the local public radio station. Write a summary of the same article you chose to be presented on the radio station. Limit your summary to two minutes speaking time. You will need an appropriate lead-in line. Read your summary aloud to another person who has not read the article. Ask that person to tell you the gist of the article.

Synthesis

Many communication contexts require that you work with outside information, that is, data that you glean from sources other than your own experience. *Synthesis* is the process by which you incorporate this information into your texts. The trick is to blend the resource material seamlessly into your own words while still giving credit to the original source (providing citations). Some communication situations will require a formal citation system, using footnotes or endnotes and listing all references on a "Works Cited" or "References" page. Other times you can be more informal and merely mention the name of the source in your text. Most news stories cite general sources or interviews with specific people. Many reports can also refer to general sources or specific people without having a formal citation. For example, if you are referring to the business plan the company has approved, there is no reason to have a formal citation—just a reference to the plan using its proper title (e.g., "Our sales goals for this product group are based on the projections included in the FY95 Business Plan"). References to people are similar: "Our assumptions about labor skills are based, in part, on our recent conversations with Alvarez and Washington in engineering."

When you use information from outside sources you have the choice of *quoting* the source directly or *paraphrasing* the text of the original. For example, assume you are dealing with a source from accounting literature, written by Terry Smith. One approach is to quote directly: "Smith states the following: 'It is important for managers to fully investigate the legal, social, and regulatory environment their companies face.'" This can be compared to the following paraphrase: "Smith admonishes managers to look at the legal, social, and regulatory issues affecting business decisions." In both cases, you would have a footnote or other formal citation for the exact source of the quote or paraphrase.

Whether you are paraphrasing or quoting directly, you must give credit to the original source. Students, particularly, struggle with this requirement. Many students think that if they change a word or two from a reference source that they have put the information in their own words and, therefore, don't have to provide a citation. Remember, even if you modify the wording of a source text, if you are using the unique ideas of another person, you must give credit to that person for those ideas. When you take the words or ideas of another person without giving him or her credit, you have committed *plagiarism*. Proven plagiarism is grounds for dismissal from most universities and certainly has no place in the professional business world either. Thus, the first rule of synthesis is to give credit to your sources. Remember, when you provide citations you not only give credit to the source, but you also provide your readers with the information they need if they want to consider your sources in more depth. Your citations give your readers better access to the information you have used; careful and accurate citations are a real service for your audience.

The goal of synthesis is to provide details and supporting material through the use of outside information. When writing or speaking, you want your words and sentences to flow smoothly from beginning to end. You want your information from other sources to seem to be an integral part of the text and not to stand out as an obvious add-on. Notice how the authors of the following text seamlessly interweave information from outside sources into their writing.

> Allowable pension costs for defense contracts are described in a general way by the Federal Acquisition Regulation System as defined in Chapter II, Cost of Federal Regulations, and in a more specific way by two CASB standards relating to pension costs: CAS Nos. 412 and 413. The CASB standards define allowable pension costs in ways that are generally consistent with tax rules, but are slightly more stringent than ERISA rules. The CASB guidelines are also very similar to Generally Accepted Accounting Principles under APB Opinion No. 8 [AICPA 1966], with one important exception: only amounts *contributed* to the fund by the date established for filing a federal income tax return are allowed.[1]

---

[1] J. Thomas and S. Tung, "Cost Manipulations Incentives Under Cost Reimbursement: Pension Costs for Defense Contractors," *The Accounting Review*, 67.4 (October 1992): 693.

CHAPTER FOUR 65

Although the text includes acronyms likely to be understood only by professionals in the field, it is clear in relating facts and ideas to each other and in spotlighting sources a perceptive reader may want to investigate further.

Situation 5: Synthesizing Information

Recent issues of the *Harvard Business Review* (1991–1993) include articles dealing with how to restructure a Masters in Business Administration (MBA) program.

Required: Research two articles in the *Harvard Business Review* from 1991 to the present and write a synthesis (with appropriate formal footnote citations) of the arguments presented.

Sources of Information

Part of content is determining relevant sources of information. Besides organizational records and the knowledge you have acquired in your position, many other sources are available.

Company Information. Most public companies are willing to send you a copy of their most recent annual reports. You might also be able to get other information such as their mission statement and basic goals and objectives, copies of company publications for their employees, for the trade, etc.

Industry Data. Most industries have trade associations that publish newsletters and magazines that provide information about the competitive environment, changes in technology, new products, salaries, and industry trends. In addition, your local library may subscribe to the periodically updated *Encyclopedia of Business Information Sources*, published by Gale Research.

Publicly Available Data. Information on organizations with publicly traded securities is available in hard copy formats such as microfiche, as well as from many computer sources such as LEXIS/NEXIS Compustat, Prodigy, and Compuserve. In addition, some of these services are offered on CD-ROM. You can find daily stock prices, 10-K's, annual reports, and other publicly available information from these sources in complete or summary form. In addition, with computer sources such as these, you can search long documents for key words. For example, with LEXIS/NEXIS, if you are interested in what companies were potentially affected by a major natural disaster, you can search all annual reports for mention of the occurrence.

Professional and Academic Studies. Journal articles and books are good sources of information gathered from studies of specific topics, companies, and industries. Computerized periodical indexes such as ABI Inform allow you to use key topic words to find potential sources. In many areas of accounting, we are seeing more field studies in monographs and in accounting journals, an interesting source for a more in-depth view of what is happening in a particular company or industry. In addition, large accounting firms are a good source of information. Often they have performed studies in a particular industry.

Professional Organizations. The American Institute of Certified Public Accountants (AICPA), Institute of Management Accountants (IMA), Institute of Internal Auditors (IIA), and Financial Executives Institute (FEI), among others, publish journals, newsletters, monographs, standards, etc. These organizations have catalogs describing various sources of information.

Governmental Data. The U.S. Government publishes a myriad of information sources about varied topics. For example, you can find housing starts, automobile sales, beer consumption data, various indexes (e.g., Consumers Price Index), etc. Most data collected by governmental agencies are available in microfiche or original text. The Congressional Information Service in Washington, D.C. publishes the *American Statistics Index*, the *Index to International Statistics*, and the *Statistical Reference Index*, all of which collect information available from the state, local, and federal agencies as well as international organizations. You may want to consult the quarterly *Index to U.S. Government Periodicals*, which lists the contents of 185 different publications.

Authoritative Pronouncements. Besides textbooks, the Financial Accounting Standards Board documents the various positions taken by interested parties when new accounting regulations are being discussed. Large firms might also have position papers they would send to you.

Tax Regulations. Tax research includes various books as well as computer sources dealing with the tax code. For most beginning researchers in tax regulation issues, looking at hardbound books is a much more efficient and effective way of finding information. Much tax research involves knowing specific jargon; thus, most people would be limited at least at first in trying to use computer sources where key words are needed for access.

Deciding on Graphics

At this stage of the planning process you need to think about the use of graphics to support or enhance your text or presentation. Graphics can take many forms, but they are always used to provide a *visual* representation of information and data, and ideally they should link your audience with your conclusions. They can help your audience grasp and retain critical points. They are more than window dressing. Next are some graphic formats you can consider. Choices among these options are a combination of what is appropriate given the data, the audience, the presentation format, and personal preferences. In addition, if you are using color monitors, color projection equipment, or color transparencies, you should choose colors that will stand up well to such projection. For example, a yellow background with white type will not show up well while a dark blue background with white type would.

Tables

A table is a systematic arrangement of data in rows and/or columns. Putting information in tabular form makes it more accessible because facts are categorized and arranged systematically. Also, tables make the comparison of several years or types of information easy. There are several types of tables, including **ruled table** (headings set off with horizontal lines) and **boxed tables** (data separated by both horizontal and vertical lines). Table 4–1 is an example of a boxed table; it includes data that are used in the figures that follow.[2]

Table 4–1. A Boxed Table

Smith Company Competitive Analysis

Profit Margins

	Model 100	Model 200	Model 300	Model 400
old	12%	5%	42%	20%
new	45%	47%	52%	42%

Market Share (millions of $ sales)

	Model 100	Model 200	Model 300	Model 400
Total market	400	350	600	50
Smith sales	20	21	210	15
Market share	5.00%	6.00%	35.00%	30.00%
Profit margins—old	12.00%	5.00%	28.80%	0.00%

Competition (millions of $ sales)

	Model 100	Model 200	Model 300	Model 400
Smith	20	21	210	15
Jones	89	92	48	2
Blue	125	31	34	3
Apex	25	59	140	5
Others	141	147	168	25
Total market	400	350	600	50

---

[2] Data in this example adapted from Dagmar Bottenbruch and Robin Cooper, *Mueller-Lemkuhl, GmbH* (Boston: Harvard Business School, 1986).

Figures

A figure provides overall information as well as impressions. Figures and tables complement each other. In a report you might present data in a table and highlight trends in a figure. Tables provide the audience with *exact* information, while figures concentrate on the visual impact of trends. At a glance the audience knows if sales have increased or decreased, if stock prices have gone up or down. The audience also can easily grasp the size of the increase or decrease. Typical types of figures include line graphs, bar graphs, pictograms, pie charts, and flowcharts. With various figures, you might be able to choose a three-dimensional option where the figure is presented with shading representing three dimensions.

Line Graphs. In line graphs the dependent variable is always shown on the vertical axis (y-axis), and the independent variable is always on the horizontal axis (x-axis). Some line graphs use more than one line in order to compare figures (see Figure 4–1).

Bar Graphs. Bar graphs also use horizontal and vertical axes, but unlike line graphs, the dependent variable can be shown on either axis.

Figure 4–1. A Line Graph

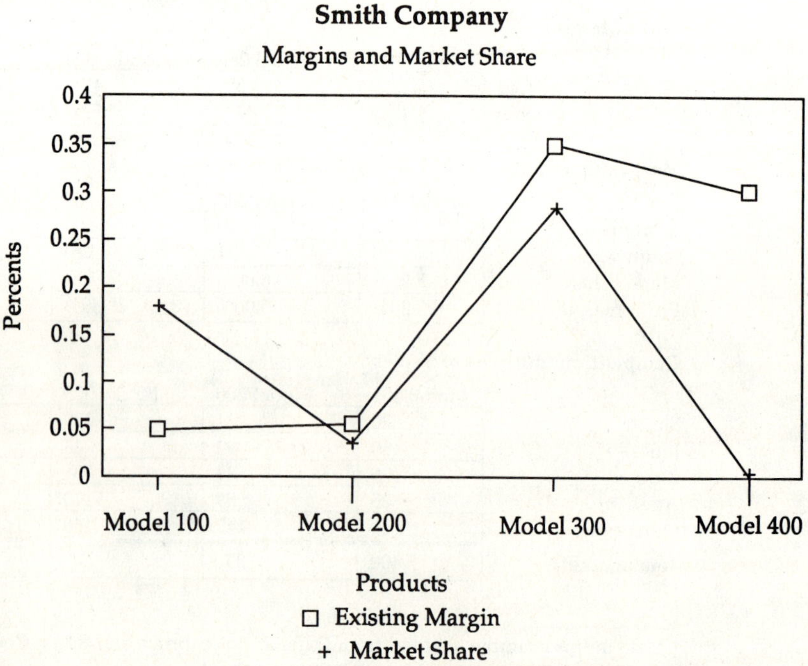

Smith Company

Margins and Market Share

CHAPTER FOUR 69

All the bars on a bar graph must be the same width; difference is expressed only in the height of the bar (see Figures 4–2 and 4–3).

Pictograms. A pictogram is closely related to a bar graph, but instead of using a bar, the pictogram uses an illustration of the product or item. Pictograms can easily mislead an audience. One basic rule is that all the pictures must be the same size; quantity is represented by the *number* of pictures, not by the size of the pictures. Situation 1 in this chapter includes a pictogram.

Pie Charts. Pie charts are used to show percentages of a whole. The pie chart represents 100 percent and is divided into percentage segments. Each segment of the pie should be labeled; crosshatching or shading can be used to set off various segments (see Figures 4–4 and 4–5).

Figure 4–2. A Bar Graph

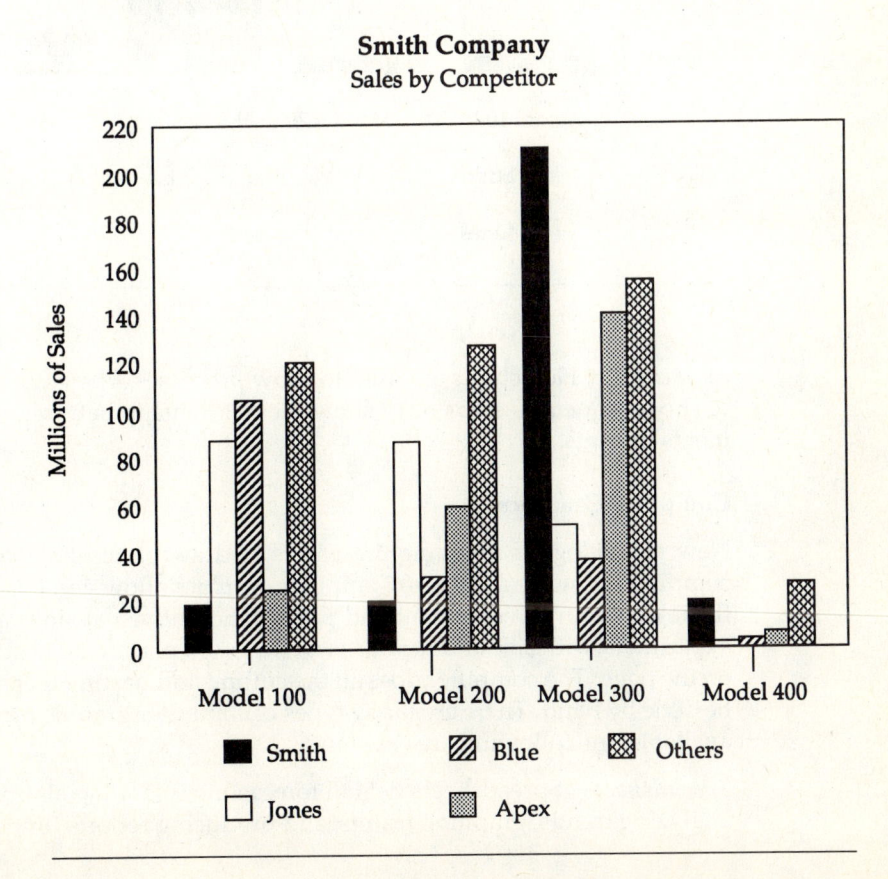

Smith Company
Sales by Competitor

Figure 4–3. A Bar Graph

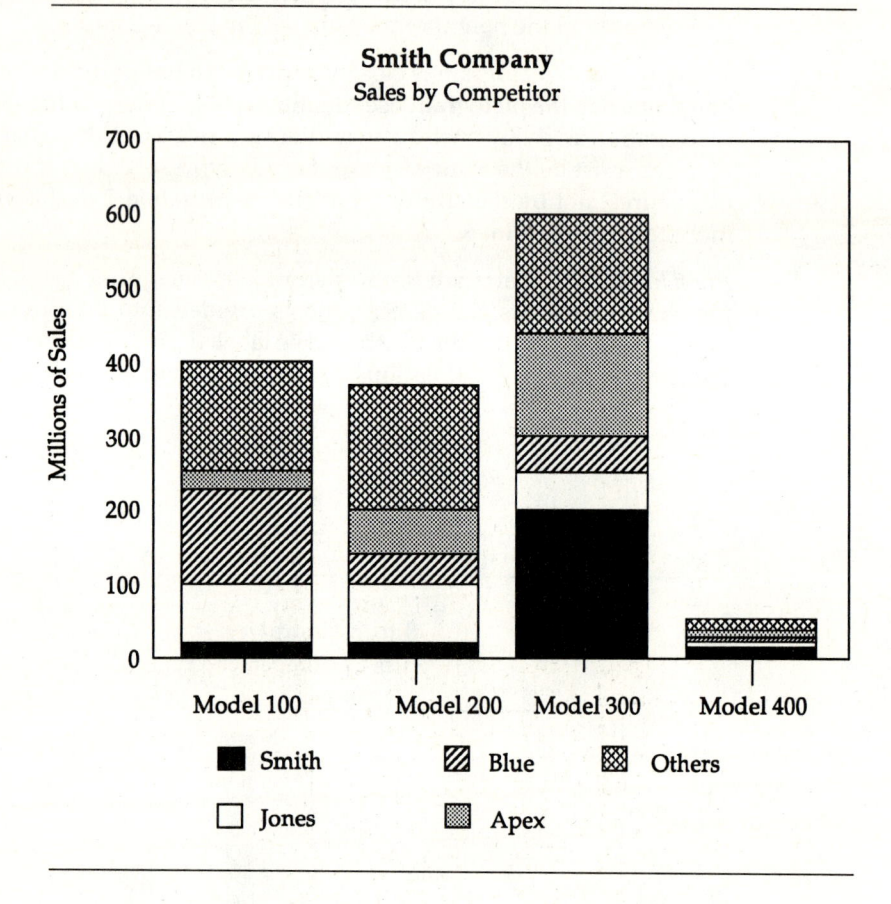

Smith Company
Sales by Competitor

[Bar graph showing Millions of Sales for Model 100, Model 200, Model 300, and Model 400, with segments for Smith, Jones, Blue, Apex, and Others]

■ Smith ▨ Blue ▩ Others
☐ Jones ▣ Apex

Flowcharts. Flowcharts are used to show processes. They can be used to show sequential steps or to show the relationship between departments or units.

Computer Graphics

New technology is allowing presenters to draw on a whole array of computer-generated images. Computer graphics allow you to be more flexible in your development and presentation of visual aids. You can experiment with size and format as well as with placement of graphics on the page. The computer does all the cutting and pasting that used to be done by hand. There are many types of computer graphic programs available; the following are examples.

Spreadsheets. Spreadsheets deal in forecasting, planning alternatives, analyzing trends, graphing results, and producing reports for decision

Figure 4–4. A Pie Chart

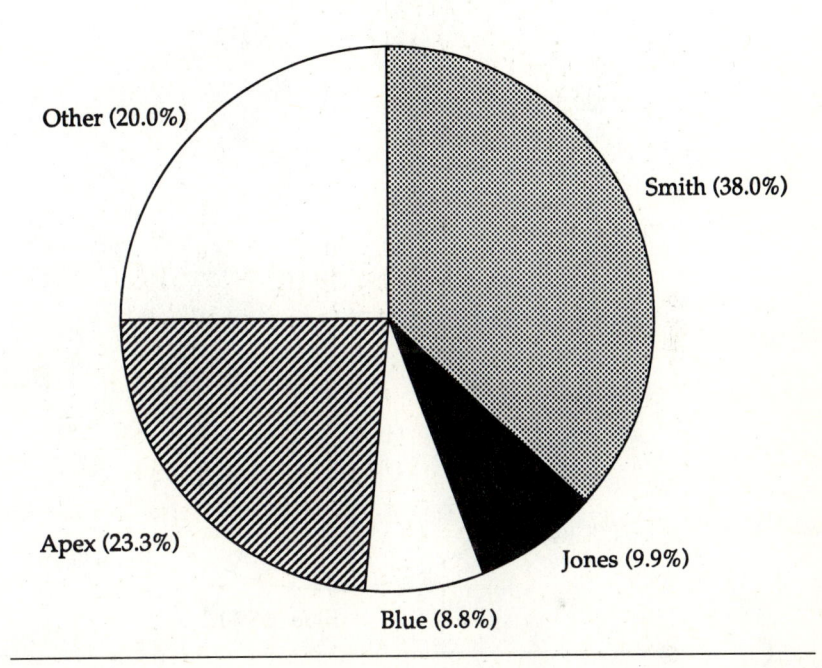

Smith Company
Model 300 Sales by Competitor

Other (20.0%)

Smith (38.0%)

Apex (23.3%)

Jones (9.9%)

Blue (8.8%)

making. A spreadsheet program also has the capability of creating graphs based on the information in the spreadsheet. However, the graphic ability of spreadsheets might be limited.

Dedicated Graphics Packages. These software programs provide more options and in many cases, better quality visuals than those created by spreadsheet programs. Most of these packages allow you to import data from spreadsheets, eliminating the tedious step of reentering data.

Integrated Software Packages. These programs combine word processing, spreadsheet, and graphic capabilities into one package. They offer convenience to the user and allow easy access to data and formats.

Presentation Software. Certain software packages allow you to create transparencies containing text and graphics. In addition to creating overhead transparencies or computer-generated transparencies for projection as part of an oral presentation, these programs allow you to have speaker notes and handouts for your audience. These programs are especially useful for oral presentations, but, in some circumstances, can also be used to create useful tables and figures for written reports.

Figure 4–5. A Pie Chart

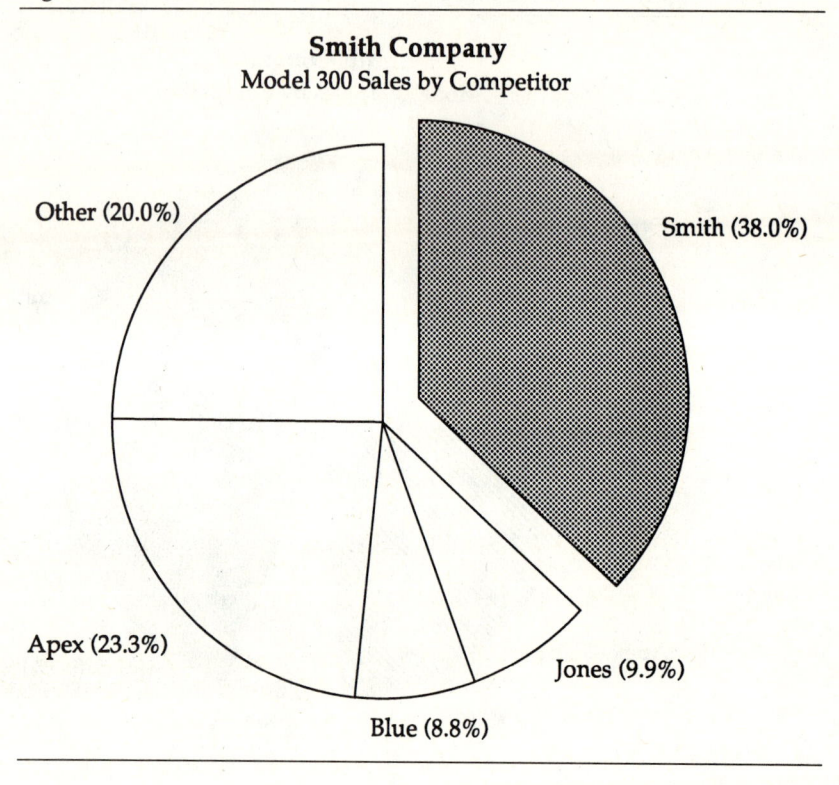

Smith Company
Model 300 Sales by Competitor

Other (20.0%)

Smith (38.0%)

Apex (23.3%)

Jones (9.9%)

Blue (8.8%)

Summary

No communication plan is complete until you have thought through and decided on an approach, and until you have gathered all the necessary research data and decided the scope of your content. Once you have decided about approach and content, you will have devised a thorough communication plan, consisting of purpose, audience, and content. You are now ready to begin drafting your text or your oral presentation. Remember that as you draft, you may decide that some of your initial decisions about approach or content may need revision. As you create the text you will probably notice where additional research would help or that your ideas would make more sense in a different framework. The communication plan you have devised is not set in stone; it is merely a formula for you to use as a basis for your communication. Be flexible in its use and be ready to revise as the communication context warrants.

CHAPTER FOUR — 73

How to Approach Selected Situations

Situation 1: Recognizing Analysis and Description

1. Three facts (description) are:

   a. Between 1950 and 1960 the number of workers using data processing equipment doubled.

   b. The number of workers using data processing equipment has more than doubled each decade from 1960–1980.

   c. In 1950 approximately one million workers used data processing equipment; by 1980, the number of workers was 11 million.

2. Interested parties could be:

   a. Data Processing Equipment Manufacturers

   b. Students

   c. Corporate Managers

3. Analysis for the three might include the following:

   a. Data Processing Equipment Manufacturers: The growth in the number of workers using data processing equipment bodes well for this industry. Individual companies need to plan to hire personnel who can both develop and build computer equipment to keep up with the demand.

   b. Students: The rapid growth in the number of workers using data processing equipment indicates a need for students to take classes and get training in the use of computers. Chances are good that a student will have to work with data processing at some point in his or her career.

   c. Corporate Managers: Because of the rapid rise in the number of workers using data processing equipment, managers can expect that much more of their business will be conducted through the use of computers. Therefore, managers need to plan on hiring people who have experience in using computers, or they need to plan on retraining current employees to use data processing equipment.

Situation 3: Creating an Indirect and a Direct Text

Direct: Our team has no other choice but to conclude Pat Simpson (V.P. of Finance) is not doing an adequate job of providing information to management. Because of this lack of communication, decisions are being made on the management level without the proper background. Several recent decisions have resulted in misunderstandings with shareholders.

Indirect: Pat Simpson (V.P. of Finance) is responsible for the generation of external reports to shareholders and taxing authorities. Our team has found that he is performing these functions well. However, there is a problem in relation to Simpson's overall communication with management.

PART TWO
Implementing a Communication Plan

5
Creating a Text

You sit at your desk, with papers and folders arrayed in front of you. The clock is moving toward midafternoon, and everyone else in the office looks busy and focused on important tasks. The water cooler crowd has dispersed already, and you shouldn't wander over there again anyway. Your PC has a completely empty screen, and you desperately hope that no one walks by to see that you're still struggling with the Midwestern report, the pet project you begged for, and the job that can really show what you can do. All the numbers are crunched, and all the research is done. The report must be submitted by tomorrow afternoon, and it will be if you can just write it up.

Now is the time to confront your old English 101 demons. Your ideas have always been creative and important, but the papers themselves never seemed to be as long as they should be. You usually procrastinated until a writing paralysis set in; today is no exception. If you could just get started, you'd be okay, you tell yourself. For now though, you just look inert to your office mates.

To this point, we have asked you to consider much of your accounting experience as a series of communication challenges, but we have also suggested that with thoughtful planning, you can control and direct many aspects of the communication process. Although communication is often complex and unpredictable, it is less intimidating if you acknowledge which parts of the process you can reasonably control and if you develop and follow a reasonable communication plan. In this chapter we will suggest some strategies for the next stage in the communication process: drafting. You will learn ways to: (1) turn your communication plan into a text, (2) initiate the drafting process, (3) begin working with your evolving text, and (4) break through writer's or speaker's block.

From Plan to Text

Successful professional accountants must understand how to turn a communication plan into a coherent message—a text—to which an audience will respond. Several factors are important to remember as you create texts for written or oral communication.

1. Remember that having a specific communication plan does not necessarily mean that you have to stick slavishly to that exact plan. In public speaking and in writing, the prime purpose of planning is to provide a foundation that will encourage you to be flexible and spontaneous as a speaker or writer.

2. Recall the main message of Chapters 2 and 3, that planning a message must include a clear understanding of the audience for that message. Time spent analyzing your audience will probably result in a clearer sense of what you want to say and how best to say it. Taking the role of potential readers and listeners, getting outside yourself, is the surest way to judge whether your plan will be effective before it actually reaches the audience.

3. Assure yourself that the more attention you give in the early stages to preparing a text, the more confident you will be in delivering your message. It is important to do your homework and consider all your alternatives carefully.

4. Understand, as discussed in Chapter 4, that the order in which you present your ideas will make a difference to most audiences. Receivers accept and remember some pieces of information simply because of where they are placed in an overall presentation, and conversely, will tend to forget other ideas placed less strategically. Generally speaking, readers and listeners will be more likely to recall what you say at the beginning of the presentation, or at the end. The practical implications are clear: (a) a communicator will want to prioritize the parts of his or her message while planning for its presentation; (b) particularly crucial ideas, facts, or data should probably be stated both early and late in the presentation, thus the importance of strong previews and summaries; (c) important ideas that attract audience interest should probably lead the presentation, while important ideas that point toward future action should probably conclude it; and (d) ideas you expect your audience to remember probably should not be submerged in the middle of a presentation.

5. Recognize that developing the specifics of a text is not a mechanical process with clean-cut techniques or formulas. Drafting is a creative act, and in some ways even an artistic one. Occasionally, writers and speakers try to force creativity by meeting the task head on ("I'm going to sit at this keyboard until an idea hits me!"). This strategy rarely works, since ideas are stimulated by other ideas. Fortunately, experienced writers and speakers have discovered some tricks that might work for you, too.

CHAPTER FIVE   79

Turning Blank Pages into Drafts

Drafting as Experimenting

Drafts are the raw material of planned written or oral presentations; in a sense, they are the trial balloons you monitor for yourself, your experiments with language that you don't need to show anyone else. You write a draft in order to come up with something better that you're later willing to share. Drafts, almost by definition, are inadequate, fragmentary, preliminary, and, in some cases, just plain bad. Since your purpose in drafting is to develop a text to work with, a clumsy first effort is no problem. You know the draft needs work before it is ready for public consumption. In Chapter 6, we'll discuss strategies for polishing (revising/editing) drafts into texts. However, at this point the question is, "How can I generate something that I can later turn into something presentable?" Remember that no one will see your early efforts—no one will know how many times you rewrote that first sentence.

Obviously, drafts are important in writing memos, letters, and reports; less obviously, they are just as important in the process of developing oral presentations. The chief difference is that drafting prose requires close word-by-word choices, whereas for most professionals drafting a speech text involves writing in outline/transition form. With the rarest of exceptions (a company spokesperson reading a prepared statement at a news conference, or the President's State of the Union message in which each word will be scrutinized by journalists and world diplomats), oral presentations should be planned carefully but ultimately spoken extemporaneously with maximum immediacy. Outline/transition drafts indicate the order in which speakers intend to explain ideas to their immediate audiences, along with whatever specific wording the speaker wants to plan for the opening, closing, and, especially, the bridges or transitions between points.

Inventing a Draft: Getting Started

When you get that stuck feeling (sometimes called writer's block and experienced by many people, even professional writers), you could quit. However, remember that until you get something down on paper, no matter how poorly done, you have nothing to work with. Keep reminding yourself, this is only a draft; it doesn't have to be perfect.

Too many people try to produce final copy at the draft stage, and end up paralyzing their critical and creative abilities. They believe they can save time by short circuiting the planning process and progressing directly to the product they want to communicate. The following are suggestions to help you get your creative flow started and your first draft produced.

1. *Arrest your inner critics.* Most of us have been socialized to think that some of our ideas are wrong, stupid, immoral, or socially unacceptable. "That'll never work," or "that's not what they want," says the critic of our inner dialogue when we first have the glimmer of an idea. Of course, many ideas in fact ultimately won't work, and won't be right. However, no idea that is dismissed immediately can develop its own life. Hunches, clues, and tentative insights are ignored and left to wither. Parents don't look at infants and say, "What good is this helpless creature?" Instead, they assume the baby needs time and nurturing in order to grow. Similarly, writers and speakers need to let their ideas breathe at first by not smothering them with criticism too soon.

2. *List all relevant ideas by brainstorming.* **Brainstorming** is a group problem-solving technique often used in business, industry, and education. Whether done in a group or by an individual, the goal of brainstorming is to prevent creativity from being hampered by assumed limitations. It emphasizes idea generation over idea evaluation. Within a time limit, brainstormers generate as many alternative ideas as possible. While creating a brainstorming list, take the word "list" literally; a list is a collection of things in no particular order. At the getting-started stage, don't worry about how unrelated ideas might ultimately hang together. Just get them all down on paper. Don't prejudge the ideas; record outrageous, ridiculous or unlikely notions along with the ones you consider obviously reasonable or possible. ("Shut down the entire division" is as good an alternative as "Hire a new internal auditor to replace Ms. Harrison.") No criticism is allowed at this initial stage. You might want to consider doing your brainstorming in several sessions, when you are in different moods, in order to tap different parts of your experience.

3. *Cluster the items on your list according to similarities of topic, data, style, audience interest, and so forth.* You may notice that some of the items you initially considered to be farfetched have some things in common with other ideas, which more obviously have merit. At first, you may have thought that it was senseless to plan for a video or computer graphics segment to your presentation, but if you cluster this idea around other listed items like "lots of diagrams crucial here," "subtle distinctions among these factors," and "audience won't like wordy elaboration," you may persuade yourself to bundle up your home computer or to rent video hardware for the occasion. All the items pointed to the necessity of a strong visual component to the presentation.

4. *Begin to evaluate your ideas.* Roam through the list of your ideas and evaluate each in terms of clarity, good sense, appropriateness to situation and audience, and persuasive appeal. Some ideas may have to be dropped because of limited time allotted to your presentation, while others, however creative they may be, are just impractical. Before

anything is crossed off your list, however, ask yourself what aspects might be salvageable. According to many researchers of creativity, the seeds of innovation are often hidden within seemingly impossible ideas.

5. *Arrange your clusters in a tentative organizational plan.* Chapter 4 suggested several possible organizational schemes you can use. These organizational strategies are common and practical ways for presenting accounting information and its implications. Along with choosing strategies for organizing ideas, you should also remember to (a) introduce your analysis in a way that catches the audience's attention; (b) alert your audience to your intended focus by a preview or presummary; (c) keep your audience up-to-date by using internal summary/transitions as your message progresses; and (d) leave the audience with a memorable and clear conclusion that, at the very least, summarizes your main ideas and may point toward some future action that can be taken.

Situation 1: Brainstorming and Clustering Ideas

You have been asked to make a presentation to upper management about the company's plans to acquire a new subsidiary in a related line of business. You have at your disposal the history of the new division, including both financial and nonfinancial information, and the analysis that your superior used (and you assisted with) to convince the president that the acquisition was a good idea. You are having trouble getting started.

1. How would brainstorming differ if your presentation were to be in writing as contrasted with a formal oral presentation?

2. Choose either format above and brainstorm about possible choices for the presentation.

3. Group the ideas you come up with.

4. Filter good ideas from those that do not seem to be workable.

5. Make a list of questions that you want answered before you can start a draft of your presentation.

6. Which organizational framework would you use?

Strategies for Written Communication

People who write daily in the course of their jobs usually develop little tricks that help them through periods of writer's block or when creativity just doesn't seem to flow. The following are some basic methods for simply getting started that have appealed to writers over the years.

Two reminders are in order. First, these methods must be understood in the context of drafting-as-experimenting, developed earlier in this chapter. This attitude is more than a technique; it is an overall appreciation that ideas come from other ideas, and that if an external conversation is not immediately available, you should invent an inner conversation to stimulate the thought process. This section describes straightforward strategies or techniques that will reinforce your basic appreciation of writing as a process of experimenting and creating for a particular audience. Without this attitude, the techniques are meaningless. The second reminder is perhaps more obvious; these strategies for written communication will also apply for oral communication situations, although we will later offer some ideas specifically tailored for your speaking responsibilities.

Consider these possibilities for increasing your creativity in drafting text:

1. *Freewriting.* When people complain of writer's block, writing isn't actually blocked in any real sense; instead, ideas feel blocked or, in some cases, the writer's mind feels totally empty. This view presumes that the mind should be like a warehouse of ideas. The ideas are stored in anticipation of a proper transportation system, perhaps a conveyer belt, to move them onto the loading dock of a year-end report or memo to the marketing department. With writer's block, though, it's like the warehouse office receives an order for merchandise that just isn't on the shelves.

However, some authors experience writing differently, and use different metaphors. Poet and essayist William Stafford, for instance, sees writing as more similar to swimming than to ordering from warehouses or reservoirs of ideas. Stafford, in his book *Writing the Australian Crawl*, points out that in water the swimmer finds no handholds, and quickly discovers that to stay still is to sink. Instead, it is only through movement and proper activity that someone can stay afloat and finally get somewhere. Ideas present similar challenges. Writers get them only by starting to write. Without actually starting, there is nothing in the way of raw material to suggest where the next ideas will come from. You sink. Stafford is right: water (and writing) has no handholds or guarantees, so you stay afloat by trusting the movement itself.[1]

Effective writers begin the process, then, by starting to write. One idea generating process taught in some classes is **freewriting**. The basic rules of freewriting are to set a time limit (10, 20, or 30 minutes are usually enough) for the writing, and don't stop writing until the time is up. If you can't think of what to say, write, "I can't think of what to say," and continue to write about how you feel about not having some-

---

[1] W. Stafford, *Writing the Australian Crawl* (Ann Arbor: University of Michigan Press, 1978), pp. 21–28.

thing to say. Although freewriting in classes is often assigned without a specific topic focus, the basic method will also work for you if you already know the topic you want to explore. Freewriting gives you a draft, though it's very rough and unrefined.

2. *Audiotaping.* For some writers, the blank paper or blank computer monitor can be intensely discouraging because the empty space symbolizes a failure to come up with ideas. The blankness is not an invitation but an intimidation. If you find it hard to generate text on blank paper or monitors, you might consider audiotaping your first draft. Use a cassette recorder in a private place where you will not be interrupted and no one will be able to hear you. If you have already developed a tentative outline for your report or other writing project, speak extemporaneously directly from the outline, recording your ideas informally. If you have no outline prepared, consider your taping as a form of oral freewriting—freespeaking. Mixed in with your idea nuggets will be some fool's gold, and you are likely to record many speech mistakes and stutterings as well. Yet when you later sit down to transcribe what you said, you will have a draft and no blank pages to worry about.

Another audiotape strategy that you might try is to tape a conversation you have with a close friend or colleague about the topic of your writing project. Although this process won't give you a draft as directly as taping your freespeaking, it will help you keep in mind the important ideas that you generate with another knowledgeable person. Additionally, recording a focused conversation may give you good preliminary clues about how an audience might react to the ideas that you eventually use in your text.

3. *Ignoring Cosmetic or Surface Concerns.* Drafting a text is not the time to polish it (see Chapter 6). Therefore, forget about spelling, punctuation, grammar, and even neatness while putting your draft together. You can read your own writing, and you will understand what you mean by certain verbal shortcuts ("cd" for "could," "w/ot" for "without," "com" for "communication," etc.). Don't start counting your words yet, or try to plan what kinds of margins, fonts, paper, or envelope your final report will sport. When you type it up or print it out in draft form, triple-space—or at least double-space—your text to invite further editing. Single spaced text on a page or screen may cause you to overlook opportunities for improvement while editing and revising.

Situation 2: Freewriting

Open an accounting book to a section that you have studied. Pick a subject from the chapter that seems difficult for you to understand. Freewrite for 10 minutes on this subject.

Strategies for Oral Communication

Public speaking is an activity that most people fear and try to avoid in their everyday lives. Your reputation is at stake when you appear before others. The public speaking experience can be intensely involving for both speaker and listeners, and speakers often feel as if they put their egos on the line when they talk in public. Criticism is difficult to hear most of the time, but for some reason, criticism of how a person speaks is often heard as criticism of who the person is. This puts great pressure on some speakers. Chapter 8 will present ways to deal with the apprehension many people feel in speech contexts.

At the same time, most executives who have been around for a while observe that those who are willing to speak in front of others receive extra recognition and rewards within the organization. The willingness to speak implies confidence, leadership, preparation, and credibility, as well as a sense of audience needs.

Tips on how to draft a speech text must take into account the extra complications of recognition in organizational life. Early in the planning and drafting stages, prospective speakers must decide what kind of speaking style helps them feel most comfortable, and what kind of role (persona) is appropriate for the anticipated tasks.

Therefore, in addition to the strategies already presented for written drafts, consider these additional suggestions for the early process of planning for oral presentations:

1. *Limit the pressure*. Since everyone is open to evaluation and criticism within public situations, decide early to focus on those things you can affect and change, rather than those over which you have no control. If you are sensitive about being overweight, bald, too tall, too short, or too whatever, that's okay, but these things really don't have much to do with preparing your speech. However, if you worry persistently about them, they may prevent you from improving the very parts of the presentation that will impress an audience no matter what you look like.

Successful public speakers have a solid sense of who they are, and don't have a great need to portray a different image. One piece of advice beginning public speakers have found helpful at times is, "Don't wow 'em." This means that with few exceptions, you should speak from within the comfort zone of your own personality. You should not strain to emulate famous speakers, to be more charismatic than you feel, or try to adopt a show business air if you are uncomfortable doing so. After deciding to do a public presentation, do a small personality assessment by asking: "In which social situations have I felt most comfortable?" "In which social situations have I felt most phoney and artificial?" and "How have I talked in the past when my colleagues have listened carefully to me?"

2. *Practice extemporaneous speaking.* As you learned earlier, extemporaneous speaking is the presentation of carefully prepared ideas in the style of spontaneous speech. It is the midpoint between total spontaneity and total planning, between winging it and spouting canned, preprocessed ideas. Extemporaneous speaking relays two important messages to an audience: that the speaker cares enough about the topic to be prepared, and that he or she cares enough about the audience to be flexible. If listeners appear confused, or even especially intrigued by one topic in the presentation, the extemporaneous speaker is confident enough to abandon the outline and make an explanatory side trip. This skill is not automatic. It comes with hard work, careful planning, and much practice.

To practice extemporaneous speaking by yourself, speak from your preliminary idea list or from your tentative outline—but speak in private where no one will hear you. Speak as if you had the audience you'll eventually address. Don't interrupt yourself, but listen carefully to the word choices you tend to make each time you run through the speech. (You may decide to tape your practice sessions, but if you do, be sure you have time to review the tapes carefully. With limited time, your best strategy might be to practice a few extra trial runs of the speech.) Much as your written drafts can suggest new and surprising ideas to you, your extemporaneous practicing will, in effect, teach you what is most important about your message and which words might be jarring or not quite right in advancing that message.

3. *Adopt a storytelling style.* Most of the oral reports and presentations you make within an organization will not literally be stories designed to entertain an audience. Yet, all public speakers can learn excellent lessons about how to be natural and persuasive by close observation of storytellers. Think about a recent conversation among your friends or co-workers; imagine that one person, Karen, is complaining about the latest shenanigans of the corporate office. Chances are, her speech is characterized by a conversational tone, animated gestures, natural movement, insistent eye contact with listeners, a tone of voice that emphasizes the important parts of the message, and moments of silence inserted into the story probably for suspense. She slows or alters her tale a bit if someone looks at her quizzically; she brings them back into the story with a few extra details. If she were asked to give a presentation at the next company meeting, she might reject the opportunity because she has no experience in public speaking. Yet, she has the best preparation for involving an audience—if she only knew how to focus it. She (and you) may not realize that there is no mystical formula for public speaking; it is simply the process of involving an audience in an important message that is expressed in her (your) own natural storytelling style.

Situation 3: Assessing the Planning of Oral Presentations

Talk with three professional accountants about oral presentations they have given. At first, do not discuss with them the ideas of this chapter, or share with them your own experiences in public speaking.

1. Are they satisfied with their success at presenting detailed information persuasively so that audiences will listen to and remember the main points?

2. How did they decide what to say and how to organize their information?

3. Do they seem to adopt an extemporaneous, storytelling style while presenting information precisely and clearly? Why or why not?

4. Do the answers to questions 2 and 3 shed any light on the answer to question 1?

Summary

Because it is an essential and often frustrating process, creating a text can be the hardest stage for a communicator to complete. It involves a number of psychological, as well as technical, factors. Although it sounds odd to think this way, creativity is often a matter of roaming freely through the range of possible ideas for any given subject, then sneaking up on yourself, in a sense, to discover what you might eventually want to say to your audience.

CHAPTER FIVE _____ 87

How to Approach a Selected Situation

Situation 1: Brainstorming and Clustering Ideas

1. Remember that in brainstorming, your first goal is to generate as many ideas as possible, without beginning to evaluate them at this stage. Your final content will tend to be stronger to the extent that you haven't hampered yourself with unproven assumptions about what will and won't work. The basic process of brainstorming, therefore, wouldn't necessarily be different in coming up with ideas for written or oral presentations. If anything, you might come up with some different ideas about how you will use or present graphs or other displays given an oral or written report.

2. You have at your disposal a good array of financial and nonfinancial information. What are the most important parts of that information that you want to present? Some brainstorming ideas might include the following as a small sample:

   a. I want to tell them about how this new subsidiary came into being—there's an interesting story there.

   b. Financial history—it's strong and a good selling point.

   c. How about a metaphor to organize the presentation? I could use a baseball metaphor where this new subsidiary is a needed addition to the team. Perhaps it's more like a good meal where this is just the right ingredient to make the whole recipe work together.

   d. Tell them about the people who work on the production floor—a loyal workforce with an average of over 15 years' experience.

3. After you think you are finished with your brainstorming, before you begin to cluster ideas, ask yourself if you silently censored any ideas as being too weird, strange, or unworkable. If so, add these to the list at this point. Remember that you do not have to play it safe when brainstorming—anything goes at this point. You want to promote rather than limit your creativity.

   The metaphor idea can be a good one to help group ideas under an organizing framework. In addition, a metaphor allows a different way to organize a presentation along topical lines.

The rest of the process really relies on how far you have come to this point. If you go through parts 1 through 3 of this situation in a complete manner, then take the time to go through filtering ideas, asking yourself questions, and deciding on your organizational framework.

6
Polishing Texts and Presentations

As a final step in the communication process, your written message needs to be revised and proofread thoroughly, and your oral presentations should be practiced and polished. In this chapter you will: (1) develop some strategies to help you be a more effective reviser and proofreader, (2) understand the role and limitations of using computers in the revising/proofreading process, (3) learn to avoid the most common mistakes in English grammar and usage, (4) learn how to assess the final page layout, and (5) develop practical strategies for polishing an oral presentation.

The Process of Revision

Revision means that you look at your draft with *new eyes*. Thus you should read your text as though it were written by someone else—a process that is more easily said than done. As writers, we often have trouble being objective and critical of our own writing. It's not that we think we are wonderful communicators, but we know what we wanted to say, and we readily assume the message has been conveyed by the text we have created. Often we don't discover a problem until we get an unexpected reaction from our audience. The audit procedure that you carefully described is performed incorrectly by your staff; the memo you meant to be humorous causes some of the staff to take offense. When your audience can't understand what you have said or reacts in a way you did not intend, you have probably not done a thorough and objective job of revising.

Several strategies will help you revise objectively. First, let some time pass between drafting and revising. If possible, begin to revise a day after you have drafted your text. Of course, in the crunch of deadlines and work schedules you may not have the luxury of this kind of time. At the very least, before you tackle revision, get up from your desk and get a snack or take a walk. When you return, you will be fresher and more objective. Second, as you revise, imagine yourself as the intended audience. Read what you have written from their perspective. Look for sentences that may lack clarity; check the organization of your paragraphs to ensure your ideas have been presented logically; see that there are appropriate transitions from one section to the next; and consider whether your message is clearly communicated. If you suspect your readers will have to struggle to understand your meaning, this is your signal to revise. In most situations, you want the audience to be able to follow your train of thought, from first sentence to last, without having to reread any sentence more than once. It helps at this point to read your text out loud, listening for awkward phrases or sentences that are too long and convoluted to read in one breath. Finally, reread the entire text from start to finish from the audience's point of view.

Consult your communication plan often as you revise, to ensure that the text fulfills your goals, meets the needs of your audience, and contains all the information you intended. If you see problem areas, based on your communication plan, adjust your draft accordingly.

Eliminating Clutter

Many accountants switch over to a forced, stiff style when they write on the job. Instead of writing sentences that flow smoothly and naturally, they create sentences with strange words and unusual word orders. Phrases such as, "Enclosed please find" are used instead of simply saying, "I have enclosed." If you were talking to someone, you would never tell them, "enclosed please find"; you would simply say, "I have enclosed." This time-worn and ineffective business writing style puts a wall between you and your reader. Since your goal is clarity, see if you can remove *clutter*. Clutter can take the form of using more words than are necessary ("due to the fact that" instead of "because") or throwing in phrases that add nothing to the communication or that bear little resemblance to conversational English. For example, "allow me to say that" is literally asking a reader's permission to say what you are going to be saying anyway, with or without permission. A phrase like this is simply not needed. Writers and speakers often introduce clutter by trying to avoid using "I" or "we." In many business communications, using the first person is appropriate. Here are some examples of typical business clutter and some suggested alternatives.

"Cluttered" Expression	Alternative
1. acknowledge receipt of	1. we received
2. allow me to say that	2. (omit)
3. as the case may be	3. (omit)
4. at the present time	4. now
5. attached please find	5. I have included

CHAPTER SIX 91

"Cluttered" Expression	Alternative
6. at your convenience	6. when you have time
7. based on the fact that	7. because
8. beg to differ	8. I disagree
9. be that as it may	9. (omit)
10. contents noted	10. I have noted
11. deem it advisable	11. believe you should
12. due to the fact that	12. because; since
13. enclosed please find	13. I have enclosed; enclosed is
14. henceforth	14. from now on
15. heretofore	15. until now
16. herewith	16. (omit)
17. in accordance with your request; per your request	17. as you requested
18. in an effort to	18. to
19. in conjunction with	19. with
20. in order that	20. for; so
21. in regard	21. concerning
22. in reply to your letter	22. (omit)
23. in the event that	23. if
24. in the near future	24. soon
25. it has come to my attention	25. I have learned
26. kindly	26. please
27. per capita	27. for each person
28. permit me to say	28. (omit)
29. please be advised	29. (omit)
30. prior to	30. before
31. pursuant to your inquiry	31. in answer to your question
32. take the liberty of saying	32. (omit)
33. thanking you in advance	33. thank you
34. we are in receipt of	34. we received
35. we regret to inform you	35. we are sorry
36. with reference to	36. about
37. with the exception of	37. except for

Note, however, that in some of these there are nuance, tone, and connotation differences that could also be factors. For example, "beg to differ" might not always be considered clutter. It is occasionally simply a less direct, and possibly tongue-in-cheek, alternative to the more confrontational "I disagree."

Revising on a Word Processor

The task of revising a draft on a word processor is much simpler than revising a longhand text or typewritten copy. You can move text around easily, change the order of sentences and paragraphs, and experiment with alternative phrasings. If you don't like an earlier change, you can quickly delete it and return to the previous version.

As handy as the word processor is, it presents a possible pitfall for the unwary writer. Documents created on a word processor look too good, too fast. On screen, writing has the potential to look neat, tidy, and reader-ready long before its time. Printed versions of first drafts also tend to look finished, especially if you print them on a laser printer. Remember that even though that printout looks polished, it's still just a draft and still needs your attention.

The Importance of Proofreading

Once you have revised your text, you are ready for the final stage, proofreading or editing. Proofreading is the quality control of written communication. Even if you have written a concise, informative, and well-organized report, one spelling error or one slip in subject/verb agreement can undermine the total effect of your work. The final version of your text, the one read by your audience, reflects on you and on the company or institution you represent. Therefore, no text should leave your hands until you are completely satisfied with its quality. This means that no text should leave your hands without being thoroughly proofread.

Proofreading is a process that requires time, alertness, and patience. Be sure to allow sufficient time to complete the process. Many costly textual errors slip through because the writer has rushed through the proofreading process. Remember, your proofreading is the last chance you have to detect mistakes and to avoid any embarrassment, your last line of defense.

Strategies for Effective Proofreading

The most effective way to proofread any document is a three-step method in which you go through the text three times, with different goals each time through. This method detects more errors and produces more improvements than a once-over proofing because you don't have to look for everything at once; the task is broken into manageable parts. You can concentrate on specific items in each stage, and you will naturally be more thorough. Below is a description of the three-step proofreading method.

The First Reading: Clarity and Sense

The goal of the first reading is to focus on the sense of the text. If you are using a computer, be sure to run the spell check or any grammar checking program and save the changes *before* beginning the first reading. Although some people are able to proofread on-screen, most people are better proofreaders if they work with hard copy. Therefore, print out the latest version of your document and do the following:

1. Read through the entire text slowly, checking for clarity and sense. If possible, read the text aloud.

2. Look for word omissions and obvious errors in word usage and punctuation.

3. Use a dictionary to check the spelling of every word you have doubts about.

4. Verify the accuracy of any numbers that appear in the text. (If possible, use a team approach to check any figures and columns of numbers. You'll increase efficiency if one person reads off the numbers while the other is checking the document.)

5. Mark all changes clearly on your text.

The Second Reading: Line-by-Line Accuracy

The second reading is hardly a reading at all in the normal sense. Your goal is to stop yourself from reading the flow of the text and instead look critically at individual lines and words. Perhaps the most common proofing problem is that our eyes move so rapidly from word to word that we often fill in words that are missing or skip over errors. Instead, in the second reading you want to slow down your eyes and do the following:

1. Use a ruler or a sheet of paper to isolate one line of text at a time, beginning at the top of your document.

2. Don't forget to check every line in the inside address and greeting of letters, as well as the headings of memos and the wording in exhibits and graphics. Many people proofread only the body of their texts, but errors can show up in *any* line of text.

3. Examine each line thoroughly before going on to the next.

4. Use a dictionary to check the accuracy of any word divisions by hyphenation.

5. Verify the accuracy and completeness of bibliographic references.
6. Mark all errors clearly on the text.
7. Make all the necessary changes on your text, correcting all errors found in both the first and second readings. Save the changes and print out a new copy of your document.

The Final Reading: Visual Impression

The last time through your text, you will be performing the final checks and assessing the overall appearance of the document.

1. Using the copy you marked during the first and second readings, check to make certain that all errors have been corrected in the final version.
2. Inspect each page, checking to make sure that the text is placed appropriately on the page and that there are no errors in spacing (e.g., a heading falls as the last line of a page with the text beginning on the next page). At this stage you may also notice inconsistent spacing (sometimes a double space between sections, sometimes a triple space) and inconsistent headings (e.g., mixing side heads and centered heads at the same level of organization).
3. Judge the overall quality of the document, including type size and paper stock.

Proofreading with a Computer

The computer can be valuable in the proofreading process; however, computers cannot take the place of human proofreading. Many people mistakenly think that once they have run their texts through a spell checker or a grammar checker, their writing is ready to be sent out. The computer helps writers check specific aspects of their texts, but you must understand the limitations of these programs; do not make the mistake of giving complete proofreading responsibility to the computer. Nothing substitutes for your own alertness in the proofreading process.

Spelling Checkers

For those of us who are poor spellers or a bit inaccurate on the keyboard, the spell checker is a boon. It reassures, saves time, and prevents embarrassing gaffes. Running the spell check is a logical first step in the proofreading process, but be sure to save any changes.

As helpful as the spell check is, be aware of the limitations built into these programs. It cannot alert you to usage errors. Many times writers spell words correctly, but have used the wrong word (e.g., form and from). These errors also happen because many English words sound the same but are spelled differently (homonyms) and many words sound similar but have very different meanings. Words like *there*, *their*, and *they're* are homonyms, while *affect* and *effect* have close pronunciations but very different meanings. Suppose you create a sentence that reads, "There examining the affect of the new cost accounting system." Since all the words are spelled correctly, the spell check will not point out that you have used the wrong "there" or that you have misused the word "affect." Thus, if you rely solely on the spell check, many word usage errors will slip through.

Grammar Checkers

Many programs are now available to check for grammar, usage, and punctuation errors. Current versions of word processing programs include the ability to check grammar as well as spelling. Again, these programs are helpful tools, but they too have built-in limitations. As long as you are aware of the limitations and do not expect the programs to find all your errors or take the place of your own proofreading, then routinely you may want to run your texts through these programs.

If you are using grammar checking software, become familiar with the errors it has been programmed to find. Most programs can locate simple subject/verb agreement problems, common word usage errors, and misuse of punctuation. Each year, more sophisticated grammar checking programs become available. Unfortunately, English is a very complicated language. The rules for grammar and usage are not finite; exceptions exist for every rule. In addition, some of these programs are designed to recognize each word as a particular part of speech (noun, verb, pronoun, adjective, adverb, etc.), but in English many words can function as several parts of speech. For example, the word "back" can be a noun, a verb, an adjective, and an adverb. Grammar checkers simply cannot be designed to handle all of the complexities of our language.

These programs are most helpful to people who already possess competent grammar skills, but who may have trouble with specific aspects. If you know you often have problems with subject/verb agreement, then you might feel more comfortable about the correctness of your texts if you run them through a grammar checker, looking specifically for errors in agreement.

People who lack basic grammar skills or for whom English is a new language are less likely to see improvement in their writing from the grammar checkers. Many times the messages given by the program are merely *alerts* to possible problems; the writer has to understand enough basic grammar to make a decision about possible changes. For example, a message that you are using the passive voice may or may not warrant a change. As with spell checkers, grammar checkers need to be used only as *aids* in the proofreading process.

Avoiding Common Grammar Errors

If you are struggling with grammar or if you are wanting to refresh your skills, consider buying one of the many writer's handbooks available, listed on pages 15 and 16. Although this book can't cover all aspects of grammar, we will highlight three of the most common problem areas that cause problems for many people: (1) subject/verb agreement, (2) pronoun/antecedent agreement, and (3) parallelism.

Subject/Verb Agreement

The rule for subject/verb agreement is a deceptively simple one: verbs should agree with their subjects in number (singular or plural). A singular subject requires a singular verb; a plural subject requires a plural verb. The key to subject/verb agreement is correctly identifying the subject of the sentence; unfortunately, this is not always easy to do. Sometimes sentences have elements such as **prepositional phrases** (a preposition and its noun or pronoun object) coming between subjects and verbs; sometimes subjects follow verbs; and sometimes sentences have compound subjects that require special attention. Below are some hints for subject/verb agreement:

1. Don't be confused by prepositional phrases or other elements coming between the subject and its verb.

   WRONG: An explanation of the figures *are* attached.

   (The subject is "explanation," not "figures," which is the object of the preposition "of.")

   RIGHT: An explanation of the figures *is* attached.

   (The singular verb "is" agrees with the singular subject "explanation." You wouldn't say, "An explanation *are* attached.")

2. Don't be confused by the use of the word *there*, or any other construction in which the subject follows the verb.

   WRONG: There *is* twenty people in the office.

   (The subject is "people," so the verb needs to be plural.)

   RIGHT: There *are* twenty people in the office.

3. A compound subject joined with *or* or *nor* (*either ... or, neither ... nor*) needs a singular verb if both subjects are singular, a plural if both subjects are plural. If one subject is singular and one is plural, make the verb agree with the subject closest to it.

   RIGHT: Neither the accountant nor her assistant *is* available.

   (Both subjects are singular, so you need the singular verb "is.")

RIGHT: Neither the accountants nor their assistants *are* available.

(Both subjects are plural, so you need the plural verb "are.")

RIGHT: Neither the accountants nor their assistant *is* available.

(The subject closest to the verb is singular, so you need the singular verb "is.")

RIGHT: Neither the accountant nor her assistants *are* available.

(The subject closest to the verb is plural, so you need the plural verb "are.")

4. Use singular verbs with these indefinite pronouns: *one, anyone, everyone, anybody, everybody, nobody, each, every, either, neither.*

WRONG: Each of the staff members *are* outstanding.

("Each" is the subject, so you need the singular verb "is.")

RIGHT: Each of the staff members *is* outstanding.

Pronoun/Antecedent Agreement

The word for which a pronoun stands is its **antecedent**; a personal pronoun takes a singular or plural form to agree with its antecedent in number. This rule, like the one for subject/verb agreement, is simple, but many people still confuse pronoun forms. We often make our grammatical choices based on what "sounds right." Unfortunately, in the case of pronoun/antecedent agreement, the incorrect form often sounds right because we've heard it said incorrectly so often. Incorrect pronoun form is one of the most common errors in both spoken and written English. Here are some suggestions to help you avoid mistakes:

1. To decide whether you need a singular or plural personal pronoun, find the antecedent and determine if it is singular or plural.

2. Use a singular pronoun to refer to a compound antecedent if it is composed of two or more singular words joined by *or, nor, either ... or, neither ... nor*:

WRONG: Neither Sally nor Martha will be given new accounts unless *they* improve.

RIGHT: Neither Sally nor Martha will be given new accounts unless *she* improves.

(*Sally* and *Martha* are part of a compound antecedent, joined with *neither ... nor*; the pronoun needs to be singular.)

3. Use singular pronouns to refer to these indefinite pronouns and adjectives: *one, anyone, everyone, anybody, everybody, nobody, each, every, either, neither*. (Avoid using the third person masculine pronoun *he* or *his* to refer to antecedents that might include females. We will discuss sexist language more in a later section of this chapter.)

   WRONG: Everybody should maintain files for *their* own clients.

   (*Everybody* is singular, so the plural pronoun is incorrect.)

   WRONG: Everybody should maintain files for *his* own clients.

   (*His* implies that all people addressed in this sentence are males.)

   RIGHT: Everybody should maintain files for *his* or *her* own clients.

   (This version reflects a nonsexist usage.)

Parallelism

Parallelism or **parallel structure** refers to using similar (parallel) constructions to emphasize the similarity of two or more thoughts in a sentence. A sentence that is parallel seems unified and avoids awkward wording. Many people ignore or simply don't understand the importance of parallel structure in their writing. Revising your text to achieve parallelism is an important step to creating a polished and professional document. Parallelism is also essential in creating lists that are part of sentences or that stand alone, perhaps in a bullet list format. What follows are some suggestions to help you recognize and achieve parallelism.

1. Use sentence elements with the same structure to connect compound elements that are similar in thought and function.

   AWKWARD: We did half the trip *by train*, and the rest *we flew*.

   PARALLEL: We did half the trip *by train* and the rest *by plane*.

   AWKWARD: Steve said that *he was* feeling ill and *could he* leave work early.

   PARALLEL: Steve said that he *was* feeling ill and *would like* to leave work early.

   (or)

   PARALLEL: Steve *said that* he was feeling ill and *asked if* he could leave work early.

2. Avoid incomplete parallelism in making a comparison.

   WRONG: Our accounting staff is more experienced than the other company.

RIGHT: Our accounting staff is more experienced than the other company's.

3. Avoid abrupt and illogical shifts in subject.

AWKWARD: A team of auditors spent a month studying the tax records, but no errors were found.

PARALLEL: A team of auditors spent a month studying the tax records but found no errors.

AWKWARD: Although the spreadsheet looked impressive, the figures were completely inaccurate.

PARALLEL: Although the spreadsheet looked impressive, it contained completely inaccurate figures.

4. Put all items in a list in the same structural form. For example, each item could begin with an action verb, each item could be a complete sentence, or each item could be a phrase. The key to creating effective lists is consistency. Choose the form you think will work best and maintain that form throughout the list.

AWKWARD: The duties of the job include meeting with clients, preparing quarterly tax returns, and you have to keep a record of your billable time.

PARALLEL: The duties of the job include *meeting* with clients, *preparing* quarterly tax returns, and *keeping* a record of billable time.

AWKWARD: Please note the following changes in your insurance benefit package:
- The deductible is now $200.00;
- Orthodontic coverage;
- Dependents are no longer covered;
- Added benefits for nonsmokers.

PARALLEL: Please note the following changes in your insurance benefit package:
- The deductible is now $200.00;
- Orthodontic coverage is included;
- Dependents are no longer covered;
- Benefits are included for nonsmokers.

(All items in the list are complete sentences.)

(or)

Please note the following changes in your insurance benefit package:

- $200.00 deductible;
- Orthodontic coverage;
- No dependent coverage;
- Benefits for nonsmokers.

(All items in the list are phrases.)

Avoiding Sexist Usage

Sexist language is the stereotyping of people according to sex and results in the favoring of one sex at the expense of the other. Sexist language most often victimizes women by implying that they are less important than men, that their interests are more trivial, or that they are limited by outdated notions of the roles they should play. Writers who use sexist language or who dismiss the importance of nonsexist usage fail to grasp that the world has changed. There no longer is a choice between sexist or nonsexist usage. Sexist language is not acceptable in any communication context. Guidelines for avoiding sexist language include the following:

1. Avoid occupational terms that suggest that the positions are held only by men.

Sexist	Nonsexist
chairman	chair or chairperson
draftsman	drafter
fireman	firefighter
policeman	police officer
postman	letter carrier
salesman	salesperson
manpower	workers, work force
foreman	supervisor

2. Do not use the masculine pronouns *he, him, himself,* and *his* unless the reference is clearly male.

   SEXIST: Each supervisor is responsible for a weekly report from *his* unit. (This is sexist unless all are indeed males.)

   NONSEXIST: Each supervisor is responsible for a weekly report from *his* or *her* unit.

   (or)

All supervisors are responsible for weekly unit reports.

(By recasting your sentences to use plural forms, you avoid having to use the *he* or *she* construction, which many people find bothersome.)

3. Alternate the use of masculine and feminine pronouns throughout your text. For example, one sentence in a report might read, "An accountant should emphasize *his* experience in *his* resume." Later in the text you could say, "An accountant also needs to indicate what computer formats *she* knows." This approach, though nonsexist overall, has a disadvantage as well. If a particular excerpt is quoted, it could well *seem* sexist out of context.

4. Avoid beginning letters to an unknown reader with "Dear Sir." When unsure of the sex of your reader, choose "Dear Sir or Madam" or follow your greeting with the name of the position you are addressing, such as "Dear Account Representative."

Assessing Page Layout

Once you have completed your final proofreading and have a final copy of your text, your last task is to assess the "look" of the text on the page. You want a text that is inviting to the reader. Memos, letters, and reports that are dense (long paragraphs and small type size) do not encourage a reader to stay with them. A professional-looking document includes adequate amounts of *white space* (areas on the page with no type, including side margins, top and bottom margins, and spaces between paragraphs) to aid reading. White space not only improves the appearance of your text, it also helps readers by giving a momentary respite. Too much white space makes a text look thin, while too little makes the text look crowded and unreadable.

If you are working with a letterhead and using a computer printer, make sure the date and inside address are not competing with the lettering of the letterhead. If you are using single spacing, double space between paragraphs to break up the text.

More complicated documents, such as reports and proposals, require additional consideration as you assess the page layout. If you have included graphic elements, make certain they are properly placed and match the text and format of the rest of the document. Charts and graphs need to have enough white space around them to set them off from the rest of the page but not so much space that they appear not to belong with the surrounding text. Make sure to check *where* a graphic will appear on a page since many word processing programs will move a graph from where you insert it to a later position. If you have created appendices, make certain they, too, have enough white space and invite the reader's attention. No hard and fast rules govern page layout, but one good strategy is to look for models of attractive page layouts from documents you have seen. Above all, be critical and objective with your final text. If this document came to you, would you find it inviting to read and would you have a positive impression of the writer, based on the look of the document? If you can say "yes" to both these questions, then you're probably ready to send your document.

Polishing Oral Presentations

You have already learned how writing and speaking present different challenges for communicators. Here we will discuss how speakers might best fine-tune their messages and, more importantly, themselves, for particular audiences and contexts.

Writing is to some extent a challenge of preparing a message almost as if it's a product; authors must anticipate possible reactions (such

---

Situation 1: Revising a Memo

Revise the memo that follows based on the context described below.

Context: Frank James' automobile repair business employs six full-time mechanics. James charges customers 20% over his cost for materials and multiplies the wage rate of the mechanics by two in determining the labor charge. Late in 19X5 James developed the following estimates for 19X6.

```
Payroll, mechanics          $103,500
Rent                           7,500
Utilities                     14,300
Insurance                      6,500
Other overhead costs          16,600
Materials for repair work     48,500
```

James estimates that 85% of mechanic time is chargeable to customers.

James has hired you as a consultant. He is an excellent mechanic, but knows little about accounting. Write a memo to Mr. James in which you show him:

a. What profit he should earn in 19X6; and

b. What multiple of labor he would have to charge (all other data remaining as originally given) to earn a $50,000 profit.

To: Frank James, Owner
From: ABC Accounting
Subject: Profit Analysis

I am writing this to you to discuss the plan that you recently sent me to evaluate for you. I have reviewed the information and have performed a cost-volume-profit analysis (CVP) to determine 19X6 profit. Profit was determined by the manipulation of the general CVP equation of Sales minus Variable Costs equals the Contribution Margin and the Contribution Margin minus Fixed Costs equals profit.

Sales is calculated by doubling the 85% of mechanic payroll that is chargeable to customers and adding 20% over the cost of materials. Variable costs are then subtracted from this sales figure to measure contribution margin. Fixed costs are subtracted from the contribution margin to estimate profit. Sales is calculated by the above stated formula as follows:
(2)(.85)($103,500) + $48,500 + (.20)($48,500) = $234,150. Variable costs of $166,300 are subtracted from sales of $234,150 to get a contribution margin of $67,850. Fixed costs of $30,600 are subtracted from the contribution margin of $67,850 for a profit of $37,250.

The above estimate of 19X6 profit is an estimate and should hold true in the relevant range. In short, to ensure that this is an accurate estimate, costs over which you can exercise control should not be changed. Other fluctuations that may occur are expected to be small and within the relevant range. Therefore, the above estimate should not be effected by these changes.

If a $50,000 profit is wished in 19X6, a 2.8065 multiple of labor cost would have to be charged. This is calculated using CVP analysis such as the above calculation of profit. Like the calculations above, all figures are the same accept that we do not double 85% of mechanic labor that is chargeable to customers. We will replace the unknown variable of X in the place of the 2 for doubling. The equation given that all the remaining above information remains the same, is as follows: X(.85)($103,500) - $166,300 - $30,600 = $50,000. When we solve for X, the multiple of labor cost needed to produce a $50,000 profit is 2.8065. This calculation also takes into consideration the assumptions above and the relevant range.

as readers' confusion and feelings of being insulted) and build in strategies to counteract or avoid them. Speaking with an audience is a different kind of challenge. The immediacy of the situation suggests that instead of preparing a message-as-a-product, your main task is to prepare *yourself*. You must not only supply a meaningful message, but be responsive and spontaneous in front of people. Contrary to some simplistic public speaking advice, oral presentations involve much more than simply delivering a dramatic talk. Effective speaking demands practice not only in speaking but in listening and sensitivity. If you've attended a poor presentation, you know how frustrating it is when the speaker answers a question other than what was asked. Here are five general reminders to help you polish your presentation:

1. *Trouble-shooting your semantics (word choice).* Consider the draft of your speech, usually a detailed outline, and do a thorough semantic analysis for your given audience. Look for terms that might be socially offensive or too technical. Find alternatives. Which jargon or specialized terminology will likely present difficulties for the listener? Accountants may readily understand the technical implications of an "external audit," but does the sales staff understand? Can you substitute more everyday terms that are just as precise? If not, then you can insert a brief definition, almost parenthetically, in your talk. (For instance, "an external audit was suggested in 1992, which means that an accountant outside the firm is hired to review . . .".) Write out your definition, and if necessary, memorize it. In addition, plan one or two brief illustrations or examples that will clarify the definition; you may not need to use these during the presentation if everyone seems to be following along smoothly, but quizzical looks or blank stares may tell you the opposite is true.

2. *Diversifying your dry runs.* Practice the presentation out loud in as many nonthreatening situations as you can. Many people avoid this stage merely because they "feel silly" while talking to themselves or into a cassette or video recorder. Presumably, however, they would also feel silly in public when the talk they've prepared falls flat. It's better to feel silly when no one knows about it. Dry-run practicing can take many forms.

    - Talk the speech through several times with a note pad nearby. You'll hear yourself creating some transitions between points that seem to work well, while others don't. In taking notes, jot down the wording that sounded effective and identify trouble spots for later repair.

    - Tape record yourself at least once all the way through without stopping, even if you get tangled up in your words or ideas. Use the tape to refine such things as your introduction and conclusion. These crucial spots must be lively and engaging without taking too much time.

- Try the speech out on a live audience that is willing to critique you from the standpoint of the ultimate listeners. Tell the tryout audience that you want honest feedback, not phony reassurance.

3. *Coordinating your visuals.* The face-to-face situation invites speakers to use several different channels of communication. If this is done skillfully, the audience will understand the message more clearly and trust you more completely. Visual aids are one means of communicating with a live audience, but they should not be chosen as an automatic strategy, whatever the situation. Visual aids should be used only as a *complement* to the verbal part of your presentation. Your new graphics software may be nice, but don't let its capabilities seduce you into elaborate displays of simple and straightforward ideas or data. Using visual demonstrations to show off your skills may distract an audience and, in some worst-case scenarios, can even suggest that you see your listeners as simplistic and unintelligent.

Visual aids in the form of charts, diagrams, or even three-dimensional models should be used when: (1) complex content must be summarized quickly for an audience; (2) striking trends will have more impact visually than orally; (3) the relationships among various components of a system are better seen than explained in words; or (4) an audience has expressed a preference for visual information.

Once you have decided which information should be reinforced with visuals, you must decide how to coordinate the visual aids with your talk. Should they introduce a problem or statistic, dramatize it, or summarize it? These are questions that cannot be answered beforehand, but must be understood within the context of audience analysis. In all likelihood, the polishing stage is the time when such decisions will come together for you. Through feedback and self-analysis you will develop a clearer sense of where your presentation might be murky, confusing, or too detailed and, therefore, need visual aids.

For example, in a presentation you may stress, "It's important to look at our company in comparison to our competitors." That information will produce more audience impact if it is followed by, "To illustrate, look at this chart. I especially want you to notice where we are dominant (point here) and where we are relatively weak." See the graphs in Chapter 4 to see how this point can be illustrated.

4. *Practicing your question and answer style.* In all but the briefest and most structured presentations, business audiences will expect you to respond to questions, comments, requests for clarification, and even disagreements. Some speakers leave no time for questions or seem to disdain or avoid them, but they pay a high price in credibility and persuasiveness. In fact, the question-and-answer period can be the most effective vehicle for you to make your point. Plan for it, prepare for it, practice it, and above all, don't forget about it in the excitement of the presentation itself.

Prior to the presentation, try to anticipate likely questions and practice direct, clear, and persuasive answers to them. Better yet, have a listener ask you tough questions and then tape record and analyze your best responses. Although avoiding and evading questions is usually counterproductive if not futile, some people suggest that trickery is the next best policy. Ignore them. Organizational communication consultant Robert Doolittle writes that he has ". . . been amazed and distressed in recent years to discover formal training programs which teach executives techniques for deflecting, avoiding, or confusing questions in public encounters." One training organization even teaches executives how to "rephrase hostile or difficult questions so that [speakers can] answer a question they would rather have heard—rather than the question asked".[1] Few suggestions could get accountants in trouble faster. Remember that precision and clarity are the hallmarks of your reputation. Here is a three-step strategy for responding to questions:

- *Perception check.* Restate the question succinctly in your own words, along with any implications that you believe you perceive in it. Although the perception check shouldn't merely echo the original questions, it can serve several valuable purposes. You verify that you understand a question. You prove to the questioner that he or she has been heard accurately. You include any audience members who may not have heard all of the original question. Finally, you establish yourself as fair, competent, and confident in your ability to explain the new point in relation to the previous one.

- *Clarification.* Respond to the question in order to clarify your overall point. Remember that although one person asked the question, your whole audience hears the answer; address everyone when you respond to the question. Some questions,

---

[1] R. Doolittle, *Professionally Speaking* (Glenview, IL: Scott, Foresman, 1988), 118.

including many unfriendly ones, give you the opportunity to restate and reinforce your own ideas, but this opportunity will be squandered if listeners perceive your attitude as defensive. Avoid sarcasm such as: "As I said in the beginning to those of you who were listening, . . .". Usually the most helpful attitude is to welcome questions as opportunities for clarification.

- *Verification*. After the question and its answer, briefly check back with the questioner to verify that his or her question has been answered adequately. In many instances, it will have been, and you can then solicit other questions. However, some questioners might remain unsatisfied after your clarification and ask for a follow-up. You will usually want to take follow-up questions, but limit them to fairly rapid clarification. Otherwise, additional and perhaps equally important questions will be curtailed. One useful response to a persistent questioner—whether an attacker or a supporter—is to invite the person to talk with you further after the presentation or when the two of you have more time for conversation. Again, keep your audience in mind: you might react differently to the president of the company as compared to someone at your own job level.

5. *Condensing and refining your notes*. Your entire process of polishing the presentation should be calculated to help you decide what you need as support during the actual presentation. Notes are important, but they can be perceived by listeners as a crutch. If you are too tied to note cards or a note pad, the chief message your listeners receive isn't that you're thorough, but that you're unprepared. Practice carefully enough to be able to decide what you *don't* need in the way of notes, text, and reminders.

Most effective public speakers gradually winnow their mass of notes and words down to an illustrative outline, which in effect *maps* the speech. This analogy suggests that the high points (main ideas) are clearly marked along with your planned route (what order you'll take them), but the special points of interest of your audience are yet to be determined by your interchange with them during the presentation. Don't lock yourself into a rigid organization by thinking that your notes must tell you the exact wording of each transition, for instance. Such rigidity will preclude the dialogue that can make your map come alive for listeners. Condense. Refine. Trust your sense of interaction. Try not to memorize; if you lose track of where you are in a formal script, you might go completely blank.

Situation 2: Polishing an Oral Presentation

You have been asked by a professional service organization to talk to their members about polishing texts and presentations. Your audience will consist of about 100 accounting and finance professionals in middle management. You will have an overhead projector at your disposal along with a computer if you want to use computer-generated graphics or slides. The presentation is to take 15 minutes.

Using this chapter as the core, prepare such a presentation. Then using the section guidelines for oral presentations, refine your presentation. You are encouraged to use colleagues and friends to be your test audience for this exercise.

Summary

Communication that audiences perceive as professional and credible does not happen magically. Effective communicators know the value of carefully revising their texts and presentations. This final polishing takes time, but the results are well worth the effort. Remember, the way you present your ideas is as important as what you have to say.

CHAPTER SIX 109

How to Approach a Selected Situation

Situation 1: Revising a Memo

Memorandum

To: Frank James
From: John Jones, ABC Accounting
Date: May 29, 19X6
Subject: Profit Analysis

I have looked over your estimates for 19X6 and have drawn up a projected income statement. (See Exhibit 1.) As you can see, based on your estimates, your pretax income will be $37,250.

You also wanted to know what multiple of labor cost you would need to charge to increase your profit to $50,000. Again, I have put this information into a table (Exhibit 2). You will need a multiple of labor of about 2.15 in order to make $50,000 holding everything else constant.

However, Frank, you might want to consider a few issues before you raise your labor charges. Will you lose customers with this higher rate? Will you still be competitive with other repair shops in your area? Are there areas where you can cut costs without changing overall quality? What is the effect of advertising? Perhaps we should discuss these issues before you make any decisions since there might be other ways for you to achieve your desired results without charging more for labor.

If you have any questions about what I have sent you, please feel free to call me. I will be happy to assist you in any way I can.

Exhibit 1
Projected Income Statement
James Auto Repair

Revenue	Materials	$ 58,200
	Labor	<u>175,950</u>
	Total	$234,150
Expenses	Materials	$ 48,500
	Payroll	103,500
	Rent	7,500
	Utilities	14,300
	Insurance	6,500
	Overhead	<u>16,600</u>
	Total	$196,900
Profit	Revenue	$234,150
	Expenses	<u>-196,900</u>
	Profit	$ 37,250

Exhibit 2
Labor Multiplier
James Auto Repair

If you want to make $50,000, you will need an additional $12,750 in profits. Thus, besides what you now get from labor ($175,950), you need an additional $12,750—a total of $188,700.

Labor cost is $103,500 with only 85 percent billable or a total of $87,975.

Finally, $188,700 divided by $87,975 yields 2.15, the multiple.

PART THREE
Focused Communication Contexts

7
Contexts for Written Communication

In the preceding chapters we have discussed general strategies for effective written and oral communication. This chapter and the one to follow will focus on specific communication contexts or formats that you as an accountant may be required to work with. This chapter describes written communication and (1) reviews the writing process and (2) offers suggestions for effectively communicating within the following written communication contexts: letters and memoranda, proposals, reports, cases, CPA and CMA examinations, and group writing projects.

Writing as a Process

Remember no matter which written communication format you choose, your text will be more effective if you recognize that writing is a process that involves four stages: planning, drafting, revising, and proofreading. We have discussed each of these stages in detail in earlier chapters. Let's briefly review the process of writing before turning to specific written communication formats.

1. *Planning*: Develop your communication plan by answering the following questions:

    Purpose: What am I trying to accomplish?

    Audience: Who will be reading this?

    Content: What do I have to say and how am I going to organize my ideas?

2. *Drafting*: Get your ideas down on paper without worrying about superficial details of correctness and polish. This is only a draft.

3. *Revising*: Look at your text from the reader's point of view. Clarify and reorganize your sentences and paragraphs. Use your communication plan as a guide for revision decisions.

4. *Proofreading*: Correct surface errors in spelling, usage, and punctuation. Also, consider the overall appearance of the document by assessing page layout, spacing, and readability of the typeface. This is the final "quality control" check.

Letters and Memoranda

Business letters and memos are the basic forms of writing every accountant will work with on a regular basis. For our purposes we will distinguish between letters and memos—letters are written for an audience *outside* of your firm; memoranda are for readers *within* your organization. Of course you might send a memo to a client and you may well have occasion to write a letter to your department manager, but these are less common than sending letters out of the office and circulating memos among the staff.

Business Letters: General Advice

Every letter you send reflects on you and on the organization you represent. Some of your readers will not have met you; they will form opinions about you and your organization based solely on the text you create. Have you ever received a business letter from someone you didn't know? By the time you finished reading the letter, you probably formed a mental image of the writer as well as some kind of positive or negative impression of the author and his or her organization. The same is true for letters you send. Therefore, one underlying goal for all your business letters must be to encourage the reader to have a positive attitude toward doing business with you and your company. Remember, too, that readers will react not only to *what* you say but to *how* you say it. A letter that sounds cold and impersonal or a letter that is disorganized, poorly written, or full of grammatical mistakes can have a negative impact on your relationship with your reader. Many business people have stories about firms with whom they will not do business due to poorly written letters.

The letters you write as an accountant will have many possible goals, including providing information (answering tax questions for a client), requesting information (asking a software manufacturer to explain a function in their spreadsheet program), requesting action (asking a client to make a choice from among suggested alternatives), and responding to requests (agreeing with the IRS to an in-house audit for a client).

Although your reasons for writing a business letter will vary, there are some general strategies you can follow. Obviously, temper the following by other factors including audience analysis.

1. *Be explicit.* Make your point quickly; don't make your reader struggle through a long, complicated introduction before discovering why you are writing.

Inexact: I am writing to you to discuss the fiscal plan that you recently sent to me to evaluate for you. My results can be summarized on the Income Statement that is attached. The results that I came up with, based on the information you gave me, indicate that your company will end up with a pretax profit of $37,250.

Explicit: I received and analyzed your fiscal plan; based on your data, your pretax profit will be $37,250. See the attached pro forma income statement for details and assumptions.

2. *Be concise.* Focus on what you have to say and delete sections that are wordy or not pertinent.

Wordy: As per your request, I wish to inform you that an analysis of information indicates that the tax regulations in France do not appear to have the same benefits as in Japan.

Concise: Based on the analysis you requested, tax regulations in Japan are more beneficial than those of France.

3. *Be precise and specific.* Avoid sentences that may be ambiguous or too abstract.

Ambiguous: We have had trouble getting a response from Ajax Company or Frank, Inc. They do not communicate with us or Jones. This makes it a problem to proceed with the project.

Specific: Since neither Ajax Company nor Frank, Inc. has responded to our letters or those from Jones, we cannot proceed with the project.

4. *Maintain a friendly, professional tone.* Avoid sounding brusque or cold. One simple way to establish a personalized tone is to write in the first person, directly addressing the reader. Depending on your relationship with, for example, Helen Corazon, such references may be "Ms. Corazon" or "Helen." Using "please" and "thank you" can also help to convey a friendly, polite tone.

Unfriendly: Our office is in receipt of your correspondence. Be advised that several measures exist that can be instituted to bring about a favorable resolution to your fiscal crisis.

Personal: I received your letter, John, and I have some ideas to help you get through this fiscal crisis.

5. *Use a conversational style.* Create short sentences and paragraphs, using the natural language of conversation. Read your letters out loud. Do your words and sentences sound natural? Are you using phrases that resemble normal speaking patterns? If your letters sound stilted and unnatural to you, you can be sure they will sound that way to your readers.

Unnatural: Pursuant to our recent conversation by telephone, enclosed please find an analysis developed to ascertain the feasibility of the utilization of straight-line depreciation.

Natural: As we discussed by phone, I am enclosing an analysis of whether you should use straight-line depreciation.

6. *Close on a positive, friendly note.* Your ending should motivate the reader to do business with your firm in the future. Depending on the situation, you might want to thank the person for his or her time or indicate your availability for continued discussion. No matter what the context, your closing should be a polite "good-bye."

Poor Closing: Please be advised that despite the fact that our proposal is delayed, someone from our office will telephone you next week with the complete plan.

Positive Closing: Thank you for your patience. I apologize for the delay in sending you our proposal and will call you Monday with the complete plan.

Business Letters: Specific Contexts

Several types of letters suggest specific strategies for writing effectively within these contexts.

1. *"Good News" Letters* (letters welcomed by the reader—awarding contracts, reporting on a favorable ruling by the IRS, etc.)

    - Put the good news or main idea first. ("I have just received the IRS report, and you will be pleased to know they have decided not to audit the New York office.")

    - Follow with the necessary details or explanations. ("The IRS decision was based on the following factors: . . .".)

    - End on a positive note by:
        — recalling benefits of the good news. ("Avoiding this audit means we can turn our full attention to the year-end closing.")
        — expressing appreciation. ("Thank you for taking the extra time to prepare for this review.")
        — motivating action. ("Now that this decision has been made, let's begin planning for next year's diversification.")
        — expressing willingness to help further. ("I will be happy to discuss future plans at your convenience.")

2. *"Bad News" Letters* (negative message for the reader—denial of a request, complaint, reprimand, objections, disagreements, etc.)

A. Indirect Approach (delaying the bad news)

- Prepare the reader for bad news by using the first sentence or paragraph as a "buffer" by:
  — providing information to help the reader accept the message in its proper context. ("Trends in business seem to follow cycles; some downturns are predictable while others seem to develop for no apparent reason. It is important to remember the long-term picture when assessing quarterly reports. Unfortunately, . . .".)
  — expressing understanding of reader's need or problem. ("I can understand your desire to lower your break-even point in new product development. However, . . .".)
  — showing you have taken the reader's situation seriously. ("I have analyzed these figures, using a variety of approaches. Despite this . . .".)
  — expressing appreciation for the reader's interest. ("Thank you for your recent request. Unfortunately, . . .".)

- Explain the reasons for the unfavorable news, then state the bad news. ("The committee awarded this contract to the group that most closely adhered to the prescribed format. Based on this . . .".)

- End the letter on a positive note by:
  — expressing appreciation to the reader. ("Thank you for your thoughtful response.")
  — expressing willingness to cooperate in the future. ("Although the budget for next year is going to be difficult to achieve, I will monitor each division on a quarterly basis to keep you up to date.")
  — expressing continued interest in the reader. ("Although your bid was not accepted on this project, we will be pleased to receive your bids on future projects.")

B. Direct Approach

- Announce the bad news diplomatically in the first sentence or first paragraph. ("After careful consideration, we have decided not to review new general ledger software during the upcoming fiscal year.")

- Make the reasons for the decision clear. ("This decision resulted from the following factors: . . . ".)

- End on a positive note by:
  - expressing appreciation for the reader. ("Again, thank you for your time and cooperation.")
  - expressing willingness to cooperate in the future. ("Please remember we will contact you when we are ready to proceed with this project next year.")
  - expressing continued interest in the reader. ("Although we have decided against looking at new software this year, we will certainly consider your firm if we change our stance on this issue.")

3. *Letters of Request or Inquiry* (Seeking information, proposals, permission, etc.)

- State your request in the first sentence or first paragraph. ("In looking through our records, we are missing the monthly statement for February. Please send a copy of this report as soon as possible.")
- Help your reader think through your request by discussing the implications of your request. ("This monthly statement is crucial to the budget planning process already underway.")
- Close with a simple thank you. ("Thank you for your time.")

4. *Letters of Persuasion* (Sales)

- Establish rapport by gaining the reader's interest and giving your reader a reason to read on. ("Every business is looking to increase profits. If you, too, are interested in building your profits, our firm has an approach that has been used by more than 50 companies in your area and will work for you.")
- Begin to develop your selling point. ("Our approach is simple, but effective—small business owners deserve the same quality service as giant corporations.")
- Consider these opening strategies:
  - Begin with a surprising fact. ("Today, small businesses represent the major hope for rebuilding the economy.")
  - Make an emotional appeal. ("The threat of bankruptcy looms large in today's world. You can avoid falling victim to bankruptcy through careful fiscal planning.")
  - Create a scenario. ("Imagine you have been asked to develop a new fiscal policy for your organization. Where can you look for help?")

— Begin with a story or an anecdote. ("In 1989, a small, little-known graphics company took a chance on an innovative approach to fiscal planning. Today, this company is one of the leaders in the field of graphic arts.")

  — Offer testimonials. ("When asked to rate the service of our firm, our clients continually give us high marks for care and concern.")

  — Suggest a problem you will solve. ("If you are like most business owners, you worry about the results of an IRS audit. We can help take that worry away from you.")

  — Identify with the reader. ("We know how it feels to watch the recession eat away at your profits.")

  — Compliment the reader. ("Your diligence and hard work have earned you a solid reputation in the small business community. Now you are ready to take the next step.")

  — Ask a question. ("Have you ever considered the advantages of working with an outside accounting firm?")

  — Use a command. ("Do not let another day go by without considering the advantages of choosing our firm to handle all your accounting needs.")

  — Show how to save money. ("Our approach will save you more than twice our fees.")

- Develop your central selling point and present your other appeals. ("Our method works. We are so sure of our approach that we guarantee you will see a difference by the end of the next quarter.")

- Close by:

  — asking the reader to act within a limited time. ("The sooner you decide, the sooner you will see the benefits. Call today.")

  — emphasizing reader benefits. ("Remember, your company will profit from using our services.")

Letters should follow a specified, consistent format. Many companies adopt specific styles, sometimes coordinated with the layout of their stationery. Date format and placement, the addressee's name and address, opening salutation, and closing should all be coordinated to enhance the professional appearance of a letter. Figures 7–1 and 7–2 are examples of two letter formats.

Figure 7–1. Block Format for Letters

```
xxxx, xxxx (date)

xxxxxxxx
xxxxxxxx (inside address)
xxxxxxxx


Dear xxx: (greeting)
xxxxxxxxxxxxxxxxxxxxxxxxxxx
xxxxxxxxxxxxxxxxxxxxxxxxxxx
xxxxxxx.


xxxxxx, (closing)

xxxxxxxx(typed name)
```

Figure 7–2. Modified Block Format

```
                 xxxx, xxxx (date)
xxxxxxxx
xxxxxxxx (inside address)
xxxxxxxx


Dear xxx: (greeting)
    xxxxxxxxxxxxxxxxxxxxxxxxxxx
xxxxxxxxxxxxxxxxxxxxxxxxxxx
xxxxxxx.


              xxxxxx, (closing)

            xxxxx(typed name)
```

Situation 1: Writing a Direct and an Indirect Letter

Sometimes James Company pays their bills on time, but often they are quite late. Currently, James owes Shasta Crafts $25,000 in receivables that are 90 days past due. In your role as a member of the accounting staff at Shasta, you have been asked to write James a letter letting them know if the bills are still unpaid within 10 days, Shasta will no longer do business with James and will pursue legal action against them.

Write a letter to Harry James, President, using:

1. The indirect method.
2. The direct method.

Memoranda: General Advice

By nature, memoranda are less formal than letters, may presume multiple readership, and usually assume your readers know each other. Even so, the design of a memo is no less important than that of a letter. Memos are usually the major way that professionals communicate with peers, supervisors, and subordinates.

Memos provide information about operations and influence decisions. Information in memos can flow up, across, and down in an organization. Memos make you visible within your organization, and your memos may have a wide range of goals, such as making announcements, giving instructions, confirming agreements, clarifying information, giving reminders, promoting good will, reporting bad news, and persuading.

Readers generally have two attitudes toward memos: they are receptive to memos that give information or request information they are willing to give; or they are resistant to memos that give bad news or make recommendations they are reluctant to follow.

Some general guidelines include the following:

1. Assess your reader(s).

   - Consider your business relationship with the reader.
   - Determine your reader's knowledge of the subject.
   - Consider your reader's attitude toward you and toward the subject of the memo.

2. Maintain a cordial and respectful tone.

   - Remove negative expressions and statements that may anger or alienate your reader.
   - Choose language and information that stresses the benefits of your message.

3. Use a conversational style, showing courtesy and sympathy.
- Strive for a balance of "I" and "you."
- Use short paragraphs and sentences.
- Use words and phrases you would use in conversation.
- Use contractions.

Memoranda: Specific Contexts

1. *Memos That Give or Request Information*
   - State the purpose of the memo. ("Our department needs the final figures from the budget committee by the end of the week.")
   - Present relevant facts or examples. ("We cannot proceed without these data, and the home office is pressuring us for a response.")
   - Close with a cordial remark; ask for action. ("Thanks for your help; remember, the deadline is Friday.")

2. *"Bad News" or Persuasive Memos*
   - Establish a shared goal or common frame of reference. ("We all know how difficult the last few months have been.")
   - Provide information that will support the bad news. ("Despite our careful planning, the new product is not selling well. We need to make additional changes.")
   - Give the bad news. ("We have decided to delay the hiring of new staff members.")
   - Close with a cordial remark; ask for or promise action. ("Although the hiring is being delayed, I hope each of you will do all you can to help us get through the next few months.")

3. *Memos That Promote Good Will*
   - Begin by announcing your message. ("Congratulations to Mavis Burke, our new senior partner.")
   - Give some significant details that explain why you are offering praise, thanks, or sympathy. ("Thanks to your efforts we have signed ten new clients this month.")
   - End by reinforcing your positive attitude toward the reader. ("We couldn't have done it without everyone's hard work. Thanks to you all.")

CHAPTER SEVEN   123

Situation 2: Writing Memos

Write a memorandum telling the recipient you will be gone from the office next week and have to cancel an important meeting between the two of you. Use the following roles and audiences:

1. Middle-level manager writing to a corporate vice-president.
2. Corporate vice-president writing to a middle-level manager.

Proposals

Proposals are persuasive reports written to "sell" a product, service, or idea to a given audience. To be effective, a proposal must convince the readers that you can provide a product, service, or idea that will best meet their specific needs. Since your proposals will often compete with those from other organizations or those from other staff members, a strong proposal should demonstrate the advantages of what your organization or your idea has to offer relative to another alternative.

Proposals: General Advice

1. *Analyze the needs of your reader(s).* Before you can convince your readers to accept your ideas or your services, you need to understand their specific needs and concerns.

2. *Know your information.* You will be much more persuasive if you sound knowledgeable and capable. Do your homework; research your topic thoroughly. Use specific examples and direct language to assure your readers of your expertise. Provide ideas your readers don't already know, or place common ideas in novel contexts.

3. *Choose a logical format.* Readers are persuaded by arguments that build logically. Most proposals follow a three-step format:

   - State the problem.
   - Analyze the situation.
   - Present the solution and recommendations.

4. *Use headings to aid readability.* Headings help your readers see the overall organization of your material. They also help you as a writer to focus and structure your material. In longer proposals, a brief table of contents (usually an outline of your first-level and second-level headings) is helpful. Figure 7–3 shows some typical headings used in proposals.

Figure 7–3. Sample Proposal Format

```
    I.   Introduction
            Subject and Purpose
            Background
            Problem Statement

   II.   Proposed Plan
            Methods
            Feasibility
            Budget

  III.   Conclusion
```

5. *Anticipate questions and objections.* Think about possible concerns or negative reactions your readers may have toward your proposal. You might want to acknowledge these concerns in the text and then provide solutions to overcome their objections. Perhaps when you were interviewing the client, you got the impression that one of the key decision makers had specific reasons why she was cool to the basic idea under discussion. This is an opportunity; use it to develop your proposal in an assertive (not defensive) manner. If you know you are in competition with another group submitting a proposal, you can discuss the advantages your organization has to offer.

6. *Provide solid evidence to support your recommendations.* Make certain your solutions are built on a logical foundation and are based on current data.

7. *Provide recommendations that address all aspects of the problem statement.* If you have listed three areas of concern in your opening problem statement, you must provide recommendations to solve all three problems. Your "problem statement" and "recommendation" sections should mirror one another.

8. *Use graphics to aid comprehension and to enhance the text.* Since graphics provide a visual explanation of a process or trend, you may want to incorporate graphic elements in your proposals. Keep your graphic elements close to the text discussing them. Most word processing programs allow you to insert graphs directly into the text. Choose a style and size that fit the impact you want. If close placement is not possible, be sure to tell the

reader exactly where the visual is located. For example: (See Exhibit A on page 5.).

9. *Use appendixes for information that would interrupt the text.* Long, complicated tables and charts should be placed at the end of the proposal. This placement keeps the flow of your text intact. Again, be sure to tell the reader exactly where the information has been placed. In almost all forms of communication, you do not want to include details such as the following:

> First we took sales and multiplied by an inflation factor of 1.03. Then we deducted an estimate of bad debts (2 percent). We then multiplied this by ...

Details such as these, if appropriate to include at all, should be part of an exhibit.

10. *Proofread your final copy with extra care.* Recently, a company asked several engineering firms to submit proposals on a major consulting job. One of the eight proposals received had several typographical and spelling errors. Those evaluating the proposals not only rejected this engineering firm solely on the basis of the errors in the proposal, but also decided they would not ask this firm to bid on future work. Thus, errors can have a long-lasting effect.

Reports

Reports can go to both internal and external audiences. They might be sent with a cover letter or memo or they might be hand delivered as part of a presentation.

The reports you write as an accountant generally fall into two categories: information reports and recommendation reports. You might be asked to provide alternative ways to report an event for financial reporting (information) and/or to recommend a particular course of action given the alternatives. Many of the suggestions listed for proposals apply to the writing of reports.

Reports: General Advice

1. *Know your audience.*
   - Determine audience interest.
   - Determine level of expertise of audience.
   - Determine audience attitudes.
   - Consider possible objections from audience.

2. *Use headings*. Use both major and minor headings. Tailor headings to fit the content and context of the report; your objective is to guide the reader through the flow of your presentation. Figure 7–4 shows a typical organizational pattern for a report.

Title Page. A title page can include (1) the title of the report (choose a title that reflects the precise nature of the information), (2) the group for whom the report was prepared, (3) the author(s), and (4) the date of release or presentation. If the report is for limited distribution, this fact should be noted on the title page; a list of people to whom the report should be circulated may also be supplied. Many companies have preprinted title pages with specific places for these items.

Table of Contents. The table of contents includes (1) the titles and page numbers of major sections and subtopics within each section and (2) a list of all appendixes. If a number of charts and tables are used, they should be listed on a separate page immediately following the table of contents.

Executive Summary. An executive summary includes a brief summary of (1) objectives, (2) results, and (3) conclusions and recommendations. The executive summary is the most important part of the report. Many executives will read only this part of the report, and the executive summary may be the only section provided to some managers. Readers often use the executive summary to determine if, and what, they should read in the report. See pages 125–126 for a more detailed discussion of executive summaries.

Introduction. The introduction to a report can include (1) background material, (2) a clear statement of objectives, and (3) an overview of the organization of the report. Introductions set the stage for all that fol-

Figure 7–4. Sample Report Format

```
    I.   Title Page
   II.   Table of Contents
  III.   Executive Summary
   IV.   Introduction
    V.   Methodology
   VI.   Results
  VII.   Limitations
 VIII.   Conclusions and Recommendations
   IX.   Appendixes
```

lows. You want to provide appropriate background information and to let the readers know what you are going to do, how you are going to do it, and what you want them to get out of the report.

The first section of the introduction should include a description of the problem and the factors that influence it. (This can be omitted if you are certain that all your readers are familiar with the underlying problem.) The objectives originate from the background information, but they need to be stated explicitly. You might even give a brief statement of your conclusions.

Methodology. In some sense, almost all reports involve research: e.g., what tax treatment to give; what software to purchase; a business plan. As such, you will have used a specific methodology to reach your conclusions. Thus, in this section include a summary of the methods used to meet the objectives of the project. Keep technical details to a minimum. Where necessary, place such details in appendixes.

Results. This section can include a meaningful description of what the research found. The report of the results should be organized around the objectives of the study. This section should not be an endless series of statistical tables. Use carefully chosen summary tables and visual aids to clarify the discussion.

Limitations. This section can include (1) problems in the research and (2) potential limitations of the data. Point out any shortcomings that your readers might overlook: for example, the danger of generalizing a local study to the national market.

Conclusions and Recommendations. This final section can include conclusions drawn from the research and stated in relation to each objective of the project. State each objective and then present the specific conclusions relevant to that objective.

Depending on the specific context, recommendations can be made if appropriate. This section is also the appropriate place to suggest additional research which might be undertaken.

Appendixes. Use appendixes for items that will appeal to only a few readers or that may be needed only for occasional reference.

Executive Summary

An executive summary is the skeleton of a report, presenting only the *essential* information. It provides a basic sense of the entire report and allows the reader to decide if the entire document needs to be read. The executive summary is the *only* part of a report many of your readers may review.

Depending on the report topic, an executive summary may contain all or some of the following elements:

1. *Purpose and scope of the report*—why the report was written and what the report covers.

2. *Methodology*—a description of research used.

3. *Findings*—what was learned.

4. *Conclusions and recommendations*—what can be inferred from the research and what should be done on the basis of these conclusions.

5. *Implementation*—feasibility and steps needed to implement the recommendations.

In some contexts, the executive summary is similar to a table of contents since it allows a reader to refer directly to topics that bear closer reading. For example, lawyers often provide their clients with summaries of long documents. Not only can the summary be used to review salient points, but also the client can identify potential problem areas for detailed discussion.

You have a choice of formats for an executive summary. Some writers prefer to use an outline form (bullet list or points). This format is brief, and usually does not require that points be in full sentences. You literally highlight key phrases in an outline form. Another approach is to use full text and short paragraphs for your summary. Different individuals have different styles; in addition, certain organizations have a preferred style.

Executive Summary: General Advice

1. Remember an executive summary is *not* the introduction to the report. It is a "capsulized" version of the entire document.

2. You can write the executive summary either before or after you write the report.

3. If you write the executive summary *before* you write the report, you will be able to judge if you have a sense of the entire report before you begin putting it together.

4. If you write the executive summary *after* you write the report, use the report's headings and subheadings to help you identify the major elements.

5. Remember to summarize; avoid using long passages from the text of the report. The idea is to give the reader an *overview* of the document.

6. Try to keep your summary short.

7. Double check to ensure that your summary and report are consistent with each other.

CHAPTER SEVEN 129

Case Analyses

Cases emphasize real-world issues and problems in an accounting course. They can be broad and include general strategic issues, or they can be more focused and deal with a specific problem. When you write a case analysis, you are expected to draw on ideas introduced in your textbook and/or other readings as well as information from class lectures. Cases help you to develop both analytical thinking skills and writing skills.

Many times when you are asked to write a case analysis for a class you will not be given a specific role, but rather will write as a student to the instructor. Obviously, this does not mirror the kinds of roles and audiences you have as a professional accountant. However, the practice of preparing a case analysis can help you to develop writing and organization skills that you will use as a practicing professional.

Depending on the assignment and directions from your instructor, a case might be cast as a simulation of a real-world report or extended memorandum with you playing the role of an outside consultant or a member of a company's staff writing to specific managers within the firm. In this context, refer to our suggestions about letters and memos (you might want to attach a cover letter) and reports (the case analysis itself). The instructor might want a specific format (e.g., requiring an executive summary).

In a traditional academic analysis, clarify the basic form, format, and coverage requirements with your instructor. For example, you will need to know if you are to create a formal, third-person analysis or if a less formal approach is acceptable. Clarifying these requirements is no different than seeking information from a supervisor in a work setting.

Cases: General Advice

1. *Read the case thoroughly.* Read carefully to get an overall understanding of the situation and the supporting facts. Then, reread the case, taking notes about key facts, assumptions, and issues. If case questions are provided, use them to formulate an approach to your analysis.

2. *Develop a plan or format; use headings.* Decide on an organizational scheme and use headings to delineate your sections. A sample format for a traditional case analysis is shown in Figure 7–5.

3. *Remember to analyze rather than describe.* A case assignment requires that you go beyond restating the facts of the case (description). You need to use the information and analyze its implications. This requirement applies no matter what format you choose. See Chapter 4 for a detailed discussion of analysis.

Figure 7–5. Sample Case Analysis Format

```
    I.   Executive Summary

   II.   Introduction

  III.   Internal Analysis (factors within the
         organization)

   IV.   External Analysis (factors outside the
         organization)

    V.   Conclusions/Recommendations
```

CPA or CMA Examinations

Essay questions on the CPA or CMA Examinations test your knowledge of the subject matter but also require that you organize and compose a solution in paragraph form. Reviewers/graders will be looking for key words and demonstration of competence within a particular topic, but they expect your solutions to be presented in clear, concise, and well-organized sentences. In fact there is a significant change in the CPA Examination. Beginning in 1994, there will be a new feature of the CPA Examination: grading of candidates' writing skills in the Business Law & Professional Responsibilities, Auditing, and Financial Accounting & Reporting sections. In the past, while there have been essay questions, the main emphasis in responses has been on using the proper key phrases or words rather than on overall writing ability coupled with the response. This is all changing since at least two responses from each section will also be graded for writing skills—and you will not know which questions will be graded this way.[1]

There are six criteria that will provide the basis for grading on the CPA Examination:

1. *Coherent organization*: This follows earlier advice that you take your reader into consideration and have a logical and linked organization. Specific recommendations include using short paragraphs (with a single main idea) and short sentences.

---

[1] J. Blum, "Accounting Education: Improved CPA Exam in 1994." *Journal of Accountancy* (October 1991): 38–39.

2. *Conciseness*: Get to the point right away. Be sure to answer what has been asked and avoid digressions.

3. *Clarity*: Be direct and unambiguous. Use terms precisely—especially when certain terms have very specific meanings.

4. *Use of standard English*: As with all audiences, your credibility is hurt if you have misspellings, poor grammar or usage, incorrect punctuation, etc. Pay special attention to this since you will not have your computer's support packages to rely on.

5. *Responsiveness to the question's requirements:* This ties in with points 2 and 3—deal with the question asked. This is not an opportunity for you to demonstrate some general knowledge about a field. Focus your response.

6. *Appropriateness for the reader*: As always, you will need to consider role, audience, and task. In this case, you might be given an assigned role and audience (e.g., writing to a client or colleague). Be aware of your audience and write a response based on what you can assume about the reader's background, knowledge of the subject, interests, and concerns. Finally, when there is no specification of audience, assume that you are writing to a knowledgeable CPA.

The Institute for Certified Management Accountants (ICMA) stresses questions that combine analytical skills and discussion with calculations.[2] In her discussion of the examination, Ballantyne states:

> You will be expected to discuss factors that can affect any business decision, such as customer convenience and satisfaction, and its effect on society and the employees. In some cases you may be asked to discuss an issue from several points of view. The purpose is to show that there are advantages as well as disadvantages associated with every decision in management accounting.[3]

The ICMA also suggests that candidates take time to look at old examinations and suggested responses. In reading, ask yourself how you would write the response in a better way than the one suggested. As with the CPA Examination, candidates for the CMA Examination should carefully read each question and recognize how different parts of each question require different answers.

---

[2] This material comes from M. Ballantyne, " Preparing for the CMA," *New Accountant* (New Dubois Corporation, December 1988), reprint from the Institute of Certified Management Accountants.

[3] Ballantyne (reprint).

Many CMA questions are open-ended; thus, you should make sure to list each response you can think of that addresses the question asked. Often the grader will have a list of ten or so possible responses, but listing four or five of these will be adequate to receive full credit.

Finally, you should use the following writing guidelines:[4]

1. *Write legibly.* If the grader cannot read your answer, you will not receive credit. If you study by writing responses to old examination questions (a good idea), it may be a good idea to have someone else read one of your practice answers. Can he or she decipher it? If your handwriting is large, double space your answers. Print your answers where necessary.

2. *Write professionally.* Don't use slang or jargon. Keep your sentences short and understandable. Avoid abbreviations since the reader might have a hard time interpreting them correctly. Watch your spelling; if you are not sure of how to spell a word, use one that you do know how to spell. Graders do not give you points for fancy words or creative writing, per se.

3. *Be concise.* The unofficial answers to the CMA examination are written using a lean style—a great deal of information is conveyed using a few words. The ICMA suggests that you practice writing in a similar manner. The length of your answer is irrelevant; graders are looking to see if you have included correct and understandable ideas.

4. *Don't underline key words or phrases.* The grader knows what to look for and this wastes valuable time.

5. *Answer the question asked.* Be sure you know what question is being asked and then focus what you write to respond to that question. You will not get credit for a good answer to the wrong question.

6. *Don't write notes to the grader.* If you cannot finish a question, instead of telling the grader that you ran out of time (something that will alert the grader that you think you have written an incomplete response), take the time you would have spent writing such a note to add another sentence or two to your response.

The core of the suggestions from both institutes is the same, as you can see by comparing the two sets of ideas.

Writing under these circumstances can be difficult. You can help alleviate some of the stress by approaching the essay questions as you would any other writing task. Use the steps in the writing process, particularly planning, to help you through the process of creating a text. In

---

[4] Ballantyne (reprint).

most cases, you will not have much time to draft and redraft. Thus, complete your planning process before beginning to write.

Exam Essays: General Advice

1. Read the problem carefully.

2. Plan your response before beginning to write.

3. Develop a key word list or outline.

4. Expand your outline as much as time allows.

5. Perform necessary calculations and check them for accuracy.

6. Write your essay.

7. Revise and proofread your essay.

Both the American Institute of Certified Public Accountants (AICPA) and the Institute of Certified Management Accountants (ICMA) publish suggested responses to all examination questions. In addition, CPA and CMA review books provide this same information. Check these resources before taking a professional examination to see the scope, depth, and format of suggested responses. In a timed situation, you want to get to the point quickly and not waste your (or the reader's) time. In addition, be aware of how each institute grades multipart questions; for example, in a three-part CMA question, if you answer one part completely and give inadequate responses to the other two, you will fail the question since each part carries equal weight in grading. Examples of essay questions from both the CPA and CMA examinations are included in the appendix to this chapter.

Group Writing Projects

At some time during your career you will likely participate in a group writing project. Many companies are currently stressing teamwork and cooperation, and group projects are a natural result of this emphasis. Group authorship has the advantage of dividing the work among several people rather than having one person be responsible for the entire text. Group writing projects also allow the various points of view and areas of expertise of the group members to be incorporated in the final product. Of course there are some negative aspects to group writing. The success of the project depends on careful planning and the complete cooperation of all group members. Individuals who don't follow the prescribed approach or who don't meet deadlines can endanger the success of the project. In addition, the final text needs to sound as though it were written by one author rather than by a group. This requires careful editing for style and consistency.

With careful planning and supervision, being part of a group writing project can be an interesting and rewarding experience.

Group Writing Projects: General Advice

1. *Set up the project.* Call an initial meeting to chart your course. Determine and agree on purpose. Analyze the audience. Generate ideas. Develop a working outline. Assign section(s) to each group member to research and write, and make sure each person fully understands his or her role.

2. *Discuss individual expectations.* Be honest about the amount of time each group member has available for the project. If you know you will be able to devote only two or three hours per week, then you need to say that and not take on duties that will require many extra hours.

3. *Develop a realistic schedule for completion of tasks.* Establish a timetable that is reasonable but will meet project deadlines. Project success depends on sticking to individual deadlines; every group member needs to understand the importance of having work done on time.

4. *Adjust the outline, tasks, expectations, and schedule as appropriate.* Conditions might change. Maintain contact with each other so you can adjust plans as new ideas occur and as deadlines are modified. For example, if a team member should get sick or have a personal emergency, others would then need to readjust the project, tasks, and schedule accordingly.

5. *Revise the text to achieve consistency and a single voice.* You can accomplish this essential but difficult element of group writing by choosing one group member or someone outside the group to serve as the editor. This person will revise the sections to be consistent in tone, style, and format. The editor's goal is to create a text that flows smoothly from beginning to end.

6. *Avoid common problems in group writing.*

PROBLEM	SOLUTION
a. Poor project management	a. Plan thoroughly and assess progress often.
b. Failure to develop clear purpose or audience	b. Discuss and agree on purpose and audience before beginning.
c. Failure to achieve single "voice"	c. Appoint one group member to coordinate stylistic consistency (with other members serving as supplemental editors).

One of the challenges of working together involves the group's power structure. In some cases, there will be an official team leader. For example, in public accounting a manager or senior staff person will be designated to be in charge. When all team members are peers, then the team develops its own leader(s). Communication among members is crucial so that problems are addressed promptly. For example, in some teams an individual or a clique "takes over" the team. Sometimes one or two people want to do virtually all the work, thereby limiting others' participation. Try to work out problems within the group. However, if you can't resolve things, members should consult with whomever is supervising the group, rather than letting the situation get worse.

Summary

All accountants must communicate their expertise through writing; composing letters, memos, and reports often dominates an accountant's work week. Your career success and advancement depends in large part on your writing abilities. Remember, writing is a skill that improves and comes more naturally with practice. The best way to strengthen your written communication skills is to write, and write often.

How to Approach Selected Situations

Situation 1: Writing a Direct and an Indirect Letter

Indirect Method:

```
                                              May 14, 19--

Mr. Harry James, President
James Company
156 East Main Street
New Concord, Ohio 43762

Dear Mr. James:

We at Shasta Crafts are proud of our service and delivery
records. We appreciate your choosing us to supply your needs.
Unfortunately, James Company presently has invoice amounts
totaling $25,000 that are 90 days past due.

We value you as a customer, but your record of payment has
been sporadic in the past. Please send us the outstanding
amount by May 24. If we do not receive payment by this date,
we will have no other choice but to seek legal action.

Thank you for taking care of this situation. Please give me a
call if you have any questions.

                                              Sincerely,
```

Direct Method:

```
                                              May 14, 19--

Mr. Harry James, President
James Company
156 East Main Street
New Concord, Ohio 43762

Dear Mr. James:

James Company has outstanding invoice amounts totaling
$25,000. These bills are presently 90 days past due.

Please send the outstanding amount by May 24. If we do not
receive payment on this date, we will terminate our business
relationship with you and will seek legal action to receive
payment.

Thank you for taking care of this situation.

                                              Sincerely,
```

Situation 2: Writing Memos

```
                        Memorandum

To:         Karen Regis, Vice President
From:       Bill Gettys, Finance Manager
Subject:    Change in Schedule
```

We tentatively scheduled a meeting for next Tuesday, September 27, to discuss proposed software purchases for the Finance Department. Unfortunately, I am no longer free on that date. The Dallas office has a crisis with their personnel that requires my assistance. I need to fly there on Monday and do not expect to get back before Friday.

I am sorry to postpone our meeting; I know how important these purchasing decisions are. I would like to reschedule at your convenience. Give me a call, so we can set up a new date.

```
                        Memorandum

To:         Bill Gettys, Finance Manager
From:       Karen Regis, Vice President
Subject:    Change in Schedule
```

I'm afraid I need to reschedule the meeting for next Tuesday. I have to be gone from the office all of next week. I know you're anxious to get moving on the software purchases, so let's try and get together on Monday, October 3.

Check your calendar and get back to me as soon as possible. I'm sorry for the inconvenience. I'm looking forward to hearing your ideas.

Appendix: Professional Examination Questions and Answers

This appendix contains some examples of essay questions and answers from recent professional examinations. The answers come from the AICPA or the ICMA as appropriate.

Uniform CPA Examination

Auditing (November 1992) Question 4

Question: An auditor is required to obtain a sufficient understanding of each of the elements of an entity's internal control structure. This is necessary to plan the audit of the entity's financial statements and to assess control risk.

Required:

a. For what purposes should an auditor's understanding of the internal control structure elements be used in planning an audit?

b. What is required for an auditor to assess control risk at below the maximum level?

c. What should an auditor consider when seeking a further reduction in the planned assessed level of control risk?

d. What are an auditor's documentation requirements concerning an entity's internal control structure and the assessed level of control risk?

Suggested Answer:

a. In planning an audit, an auditor's understanding of the internal control structure elements should be used to identify the types of potential misstatements that could occur, to consider the factors affecting the risk of material misstatement, and to influence the design of substantive tests.

b. An auditor obtains an understanding of the design of relevant internal control structure policies and procedures and whether they have been placed in operation. Assessing control risk at below the maximum level further involves identifying specific policies and procedures relevant to specific assertions that are likely to prevent or detect material misstatements in those assertions. It also involves performing tests of control to evaluate the operating design and effectiveness of such policies and procedures.

c. When seeking a further reduction in the assessed level of control risk, an auditor should consider whether additional evidential matter sufficient to support a further reduction is likely to be available, and whether it would be efficient to perform tests of controls to obtain that evidential matter.

d. An auditor should document the understanding of an entity's internal control structure elements obtained to plan the audit. The auditor also should document the basis for the auditor's conclusion about the assessed level of control risk. If control risk is assessed at the maximum level, the auditor should document that conclusion, but is not required to document the basis for that conclusion. However, if the assessed level of control risk is below the maximum level, the auditor should document the basis for the conclusion that the effectiveness of the design and the operation of internal control structure policies and procedures supports that assessed level.

(AICPA, reprinted)

Some Notes: The role, audience, and task for this question involve you as a candidate writing to the person who will assess your response to the specific questions asked. Under the 1994 guidelines, your reader is a knowledgeable CPA. You will want to get right to the point, avoid repeating the question, and make sure that you cover all the aspects of each part of the question asked. Please note that the suggested response covers all the parts of the question that the examiners want covered; you can word these responses in your own style.

Accounting Theory (November 1992) Number 5

Question: Winter Sports Co. rents winter sports equipment to the public. Snowmobiles are depreciated by the double declining balance method. Before the season began, the estimated lives of several snowmobiles were extended because engines were replaced. Winter was given thirty days to pay for the engines. Winter gave the old engines to a local mechanic who agreed to provide repairs and maintenance service in the next year equal to the fair market value of the engines. Rental skis, poles, and boots are capitalized and depreciated according to the inventory (appraisal) method.

Required:

a. How would Winter account for the purchase of the new engines and the transfer of the old engines to the local mechanic if the old engines' costs are

1. Known?

2. Unknown?

b. 1. What are two assumptions underlying use of an accelerated depreciation method?

   2. How should Winter calculate the snowmobiles' depreciation?

c. How should Winter calculate and report the costs of the skis, poles, and boots in its balance sheets and income statements?

Suggested Answer:

a. 1. When the old engines' costs are known, the snowmobiles account is decreased by the old engines' costs, and accumulated depreciation is decreased by the accumulated depreciation on the old engines. A current asset would be recorded for the fair market value of the future repair and maintenance services. The net difference between the old engines' carrying amounts and their fair values is recorded as an operating gain or loss. To record the new engines' acquisition, both the snowmobiles account and the accounts payable are increased by the new engines' costs.

   2. If the old engines' costs are unknown then either the snowmobiles account would be increased or accumulated depreciation would be decreased by the difference between the new engines' costs and the old engines' fair value.

b. 1. Assumptions underlying the use of an accelerated depreciation method include:

   - An asset is more productive in the earlier years of its estimated useful life. Therefore, greater depreciation charges in the earlier years would be matched against the greater revenues generated in the earlier years.

   - Repair and maintenance costs are often higher in later periods and an accelerated depreciation method results in a more nearly annual constant total cost over the years of use.

   - An asset may become obsolete before the end of its originally estimated useful life. The risk associated with estimated long-term cash flows is greater than the risk associated with near-term cash flows. Accelerated depreciation recognizes this condition.

   2. Winter should calculate snowmobile depreciation by applying twice the straight-line rate to their carrying amounts.

c. Under the investor (appraisal) method, Winter calculates the ending undepreciated cost on the skis, poles, and boots by multiplying the physical quantities of these items on hand by an appraised amount. This ending undepreciated cost is classified as a noncurrent asset. Depreciation included in continuing operations equals the sum of the beginning balance and purchases for the year, less the ending undepreciated cost.

(AICPA, reprinted)

Some Notes: Look back at the question and answer to part a. Note that almost all the information in the basic part of the question comes into play in the response. Make sure that you are covering all the issues brought up by the question. While you should watch out for extraneous information, odds are that almost all of what is offered in the basic part of the question has use somewhere in the answer.

Certified Management Accountant Examination

Part 3 (December 1992) Question 4

Question: Extra Strength Materials (ESM) is a four-year-old company founded by Art Mallory and several associates who developed a process to produce steel-like strength materials of lighter weights than traditional steels and plastics. With government pressure on the automobile industry to produce vehicles capable of higher gas mileage, ESM has had some success in penetrating the automobile industry.

ESM's management and employees have operated in an entrepreneurial spirit, pursuing manufacturing process changes and markets with few controls on spending. As the costs of operations have been exceeding revenues during this start-up phase, ESM recently sought an established partner with the financial resources to expand the company. Mid-America Steel Inc., seeking to diversify its business, bought ESM with the understanding that it would continue to operate as an independent subsidiary with existing management running the company. However, Mid-America's corporate headquarters would exercise oversight of ESM's operations.

Dave Johnson, chief financial officer of Mid-America, requested that his staff review ESM's financial reporting system. They note that, in accordance with the entrepreneurial culture, the overall company budget was developed each year by Mallory and his controller so that his staff could concentrate on production, research, and marketing. With the anticipated growth of ESM, Johnson recommended to Mallory that ESM adopt and implement a departmental budgeting system. Mallory announced to his associates and departmental managers that ESM was planning to accept Johnson's recommendation.

Johnson's budget director presented to ESM's managers an overview of the departmental budgeting system and the participation in the process that would be expected of them. Mallory then requested the managers to review the procedures and make suggestions regarding the implementation of the budgeting system. Mallory further advised that since this would be their first exposure to budgeting with ESM, they should raise any questions they might have with regards to budgeting and how operations would be conducted as a result of the changeover.

Required:

a. Describe benefits, other than better cost control, that are likely to accrue to ESM from the implementation of departmental budgeting.

b. Discuss the behavioral issues that the introduction of a departmental budgeting system is likely to raise with ESM's department managers.

c. Discuss the behavioral issues that the introduction of a departmental budgeting system is likely to raise with ESM's production workers.

d. Discuss the likely reactions of ESM's employees after several months of being confronted with the pressure of comparing actual results to budgeted expectations.

Suggested Answer:

a. The benefits, other than better cost control, that are likely to accrue to Extra Strength Materials (ESM) from the implementation of departmental budgeting include

- improved communications and coordination among departments.
- earlier identification of problems and/or potential company weaknesses.
- better definition of accountability (responsibility accounting) and performance expectations.

b. The behavioral issues that the introduction of a departmental budgeting system is likely to raise with ESM's department managers may be both positive and negative.

Positive issues are likely to include

- increased motivation to achieve budgets if they are perceived as attainable.
- acceptance of the risks and rewards associated with budget accountability.
- acceptance of performance evaluations if budgeting was participative.

Negative issues may include

- fear of punishment if budgets are not achieved.
- fear of loss of control and authority.
- confusion over the options of achieving the budget vs. schedule vs. quality.

c. The behavioral issues that the introduction of a departmental budgeting system is likely to raise with ESM's production workers may be both positive and negative.

Positive issues are likely to include

- acceptance of performance evaluations based on attainable budget expectations.
- a sense of commitment and ownership if they participate in the budget-setting process.

Negative issues are likely to include

- fear of punishment for not achieving goals.
- fear that greater control could lead to loss of jobs.
- sabotage of the budgeting system or giving up if it is perceived that budgets are not attainable.

d. The likely reactions of ESM's employees after several months' experience with actual vs. budget include the following.

- If objectives are not attained, employees could
  - see them as unrealistic and become negative or ignore budgets.
  - become stressed and adversely affect performance evaluations.
- If employees feel objectives are/were attainable, they could
  - increase motivation by fostering a spirit to improve operations if they participated in the budgeting process.
  - foster a feeling of partnership with management in achieving results.
- View management as the enemy.
- Perceive a feeling of more control over their jobs since job direction and constraints are well defined; however, employees may also have fears of job loss due to the increased control.

(ICMA, reprinted)

Some Notes: The suggested responses from the ICMA are worded in the manner you see above. There is the implicit role and audience here of the candidate and the grader of the examination since nothing else is stated and the questions are all worded from that point of view. As with our suggestions with the CPA Examination, be direct and cover all the necessary points. You can choose a bullet-point format as illustrated previously as long as you put an adequate introduction to each list of items.

Part 1 (June 1992) Question 4

Question: Barnes Inc. manufactures a line of games and toys that is sold to discount stores and retail outlets. The company has several thousand credit customers, and Sally Johnson, Barnes' treasurer, is concerned about the company's current credit and collection policies. Barnes' current credit terms are 2/15, net 45, which are in line with industry practices. Johnson's office is responsible for collections. Past due invoices carry a notice regarding delinquencies, and phone calls are made to follow up on delinquent payments over $5,000; invoices greater than six months overdue are given to a collection agency.

After evaluating various alternatives, Johnson has decided to implement the following changes to Barnes' policies.

- The credit terms extended to customers will be changed to 2/10, net 30. Johnson believes that this change will have little effect on sales as current customers will quickly become accustomed to the new requirements, and new customers will accept the terms as part of Barnes' overall policies. The overall effect of this change will be to increase accounts receivable turnover and reduce the opportunity cost of carrying outstanding receivables.

- Collection efforts will be increased to ensure better compliance with the new credit terms. All invoices over 30 days will carry notification that failure to pay within the next 60 days will incur interest charges of 1.5 percent per month. Phone calls will be made on all overdue accounts in excess of $2,000, and invoices over 120 days past due will be turned over to the collection agency. Johns believes that these efforts could reduce the write-off of bad debts by as much as $100,000.

Bob Redman, Barnes' sales manager, is responsible for granting credit to prospective customers and adjusting credit limits to fit customers' needs. Redman has a network of approximately 50 sales representatives through whom Barnes' products are sold, and he has extended credit granting privileges to the majority of these representatives. Redman's philosophy is that as long as there is available production capacity, Barnes should sell to anyone who wants to stock its products. If he is more lenient with a few new customers, it will not affect the current customer base.

Johnson sent the following memorandum to Redman regarding the changes she has made.

```
To:        Bob Redman
From:      Sally Johnson
Subject:   Credit and Collection Policies

In an effort to increase receivables turnover,
reduce the write-off of bad debts, and avoid
unwarranted opportunity costs, the company's
credit terms have been changed to 2/10, net 30.
In addition, stepped-up collection efforts
could save the company $100,000. In view of the
fact that poor collections resulting from de-
viations from established policies will reflect
on your department, you may wish to review your
credit granting procedures.
```

Required:

a. By describing the probable effects of the changes made to Barnes Inc.'s credit and collection policies, evaluate Sally Johnson's decision to change

1. credit terms.
2. collection procedures.

b. Bob Redman's credit granting philosophy appears to be in conflict with Sally Johnson's efforts.

1. Describe the likely effects of Redman's credit granting philosophies.
2. Explain the possible pitfalls in Redman's philosophy regarding the granting of credit.

c. 1. Evaluate Sally Johnson's memorandum as a communication device.
2. Describe Bob Redman's probable reaction to Sally Johnson's memorandum.

Suggested Answer:

a. 1. The change in credit terms implemented by Sally Johnson is likely to have the following effects.

- The change in terms may cause a loss of sales because
  - the terms are more stringent than industry standards which may cause customers to switch to competitors with more relaxed terms.
  - new customers may not be willing to accept stricter terms.
- The number of past due invoices is likely to increase as the payment period is shortened.
- Some cash may flow earlier as customers meet the new discount period and the 30-day payment period.

2. The new collection procedures could have the following effects.

- Current customers are likely to be irritated by the new procedures, particularly those that have been taking 45 days to pay and those with $2,000–$5,000 balances.
- The new procedures may speed collections and reduce accounts receivable balances as it appears that procedures have been lax and poorly controlled in the past.

b. 1. Bob Redman's credit granting policy will most likely increase Barnes' sales but is also likely to have the following adverse effects.

- A portion of the new customers are likely to default, increasing bad debt expense.
- Collections are likely to slow, reducing cash flow.
- Current customers may relax payment schedules when they learn that credit requirements have been relaxed for others.

2. The possible pitfalls in Bob Redman's credit granting philosophy include the following.

- The profit margin associated with the increased sales may not be sufficient to cover the increased costs of collection and default.
- The continual sale of products to customers with minimal capabilities to pay may jeopardize the future of the company because of decreased cash flows.

c. 1. Other than having the advantage of being a written permanent document, Sally Johnson's memorandum is deficient as a communication device on several levels, including the following.

- The memorandum is too short, and the tone is confrontational.
- The memo does not provide any explanation for the changes.
- It appears that there was no consideration of the effect the changes would have on company sales.
- Johnson has used accounting jargon which will not aid Redman's understanding of the situation.

2. Bob Redman's probable reaction to Sally Johnson's memorandum is likely to be negative. He has not been asked to participate in making this change and is likely to feel that no consideration has been given to his responsibilities. Any existing relationship between Redman and Johnson will deteriorate as Redman is unlikely to change his thinking about granting credit.

(ICMA, reprinted)

Some Notes: It's interesting that the ICMA is asking you to evaluate Johnson's memorandum. Note their concerns as they mirror some of the ideas we explore—you must consider your audience when planning to write such a memorandum. She has described without explaining or analyzing things for her reader. Her memorandum is direct, but too blunt and confrontational. She misjudges her audience by using jargon.

8
Contexts for Oral Communication

Francine Fiscal and a team of two other accountants have spent over a month researching the economic implications of closing the Dayton plant. The group met four times last week to discuss their recommendations, and how they should be written up. They decided on the report's organization, format, and even the type of binding most appropriate for delivering the manuscript to upper management.

Fiscal spent over 20 hours at work and at home drafting the text, and another six or seven hours revising it after her colleagues' close reading and careful feedback. The report, finally ready, is on the boss's desk two days in advance of its Friday deadline. It is an imposing achievement: 82 pages of data, interpretations, charts, and recommendations supplemented by several appendices of policies and precedents. The team of accountants is justifiably proud of it.

Late Wednesday afternoon each of the three accountants receives a memo requesting a twenty-minute "presentation of findings" to company executives on Monday morning in the conference room. In commiserating, they can't decide whether this is because the executives are lazy and don't want to read the entire report or whether they are severely pressed for time and want to know firsthand what the team thinks is the nitty-gritty material in the document. It doesn't matter. A project that has consumed five months of their time is now about to consume five more days. Its ultimate success will depend upon a mere twenty minutes. Therefore, the upcoming five days in the life of the project are just as crucial as the preceding five months.

A large percentage of today's executives are relying more and more on oral presentations. One business executive estimates that 33 million corporate presentations are given each *day*. Xerox estimates that *70 percent* of a typical executive's time is spent in meetings.[1] This doesn't leave much time for reading 80-page reports carefully. No wonder executives

---
[1] R. Hoff, *"I Can See You Naked": A Fearless Guide to Making Great Presentations* (Kansas City, MO: Andrews and McMeel, 1988) pp. 30, 138.

would want to (a) hear only those facts and recommendations they need to hear, (b) streamline meetings they need to have, and, therefore, (c) encourage ever more concise presentations by others.

In other words, the report is for the files and perhaps for reference; *the presentation is often the genuine basis for the decision-making*. Will Francine Fiscal and her colleagues use the next five days wisely? They will, if they heed advice found in this chapter. First, we discuss one overall problem that is variously labeled stage fright, nervousness, shyness, and, more recently, communication apprehension. In whatever guise, fear keeps many talented people from achieving recognition and success that is rightfully theirs. If Fiscal and her co-workers are immobilized by nervousness at a face-to-face presentation and fail to use the next five days efficiently, much of their earlier good work will be wasted. The impact of an organizational report may actually reside less in its content than in its presentation.

Second, we look at oral communication competence in two very common organizational contexts: (1) highly structured individual and group presentations in which you justify information and interpretations to decision makers, and (2) interviews with knowledgeable people in which you elicit essential information for the presentation you're planning.

Communication Apprehension: Nervousness Is Normal

Imagine that you are in the conference room to hear Francine Fiscal's team present their recommendations. Although facts and figures are very important, you will also implicitly evaluate how strongly the team feels about its recommendations, and how confident they are about their projections. The most reliable clues people use to evaluate feelings and moods are contained in the *nonverbal* communication realm.

One expert in nonverbal interaction estimates that most impressions of personality and effectiveness are gained by listeners *within the first four minutes* of meeting someone.[2] This situation shocks some people when they learn about it. This isn't fair, they think; surely we give each other more slack than that. The answer is that at the conscious level, we often give plenty of opportunities, but at the unconscious level, we reach conclusions rapidly on the basis of nonverbal cues, conclusions that are difficult to revise. Therefore, speakers like Francine must be aware that at the time when she and her colleagues are likely to be most nervous and exhibit the most obvious symptoms of apprehension, the audience is most primed to notice these symptoms. In addition, symptoms of nervousness are often interpreted to mean that speakers are not confi-

---

[2] L. Zunin, *Contact: The First Four Minutes* (New York, NY: Ballantine, 1972).

dent about their content, do not feel strongly about their ideas, or (perhaps worse) are not prepared.

However, effective speakers can anticipate these potential hot spots of presentations and sidestep at least some of them. As with most basic competencies, there are two elementary considerations to improving presentational confidence: what to know, and what to do. Because entire books[3] are available to instruct you on avoiding stage fright, we will only skim the surface. However, consider the following checklist, containing suggestions supported by years of practical experience and research into public speaking.

What to Know and Understand About Communication Apprehension

1. *Nervousness is normal and healthy.* When you're nervous it often seems as if other people would be perfectly comfortable in the same situation. However, this is usually not the case. Nervousness is widespread, natural, and healthy; it is your signal that what you're about to do is important. Think about the tasks of your life—such as ordering lunch at a cafe, choosing dishwashing soap at the grocery store, or driving your normal route to work—and you'll realize that you're not nervous doing them. When you're nervous, it's because how people speak and listen face to face can have an impact on their decisions and maybe their lives. If managed properly, it energizes you and can raise your alertness and performance to the demands of each new challenge. The key is the phrase, "if managed properly."

2. *Nervousness can be managed.* You want the optimum amount of nervous energy for your presentation. Too much, and listeners believe you're less competent. Too little, and listeners believe you're less enthusiastic or committed. Research shows that speakers can control apprehension signals significantly through some relatively simple reminders and techniques. We'll consider these later in this chapter.

3. *Nervousness diminishes with practice and confidence.* Once you feel in command of your material and have rehearsed a presentation thoroughly, and once you've anticipated the range of possible reactions from your audience, you may experience less apprehension. At the very least, your apprehension will be of the energizing variety, easily channeled into the enthusiasm any presentation needs.

4. *Nervousness varies with self-consciousness.* Many speakers suffer from the "How Am I Doing?" syndrome. Instead of concentrating on their enthusiasm for their subject matter and how well the audience is

---

[3] For example, see R. Nelson, *Louder and Funnier: A Practical Guide for Overcoming Stagefright in Speechmaking* (Berkeley, CA: Ten Speed Press, 1985).

understanding their presentation, they focus their fears somewhat selfishly on themselves. Effective speakers realize that their subjects and audiences are much more important in the grand scheme of things than their own personal reputations. Ironically, these persons usually emerge from their presentations with solid reputations, precisely because reputation wasn't their all-consuming worry.

5. *Nervousness is rarely as obvious to an audience as it is to an apprehensive speaker.* Unfortunately, many presenters use their internal jitters falsely as a signal of their imagined external failures. In other words, your knees may shake and you feel a quaver in your voice that isn't normally there. Your hands feel clammy, and there's a bead of sweat on your forehead. You fantasize the audience *must* be focusing on these things, and are ready to dismiss you as a fool or a beginner. Remind yourself that in almost all speaking situations, such signs will be either unnoticeable or inconsequential to audiences. If *you* focus on them, you only distract yourself from your genuine goals—and increase the chances of making mistakes that will truly make everyone more uncomfortable.

If you can remember such reminders about the nature of nervousness, you are ready to practice some behavioral changes that will help you manage your nervousness. Not all techniques will work for everyone, of course; you'll have to experiment with several of them to personalize what works for you.

What to Do About Communication Apprehension

1. *Prepare thoroughly.* It's amazing how many speakers believe they're hampered by nervousness when in fact they are hampered by their own lack of preparation. The nervousness they subsequently feel is justified—they should be scared. Adequate topic research, audience analysis, and goal setting can remove or diminish this type of unnecessary problem. Focus on your content and audience. Remind yourself constantly: "I'm personally not as important as this policy change" (or the image of the company, or the profits for next quarter, etc.).

2. *Rehearse your content and style.* This simple advice applies to all presentations, and applies even to presenters who have no friends around to critique them. The more you practice the presentation, the more you're teaching yourself about alternative wordings, what sounds good, what makes more sense, and the like. Of course, ideally you will receive feedback on your rehearsals before the presentation itself. It's not as useful to try to rehearse the whole presentation all the way through as it is to divide it into manageable

bits and practice those. As you learn to control the presentation's various sections individually, they will seem more like pieces that fit together to complete a coherent picture, rather than an unassembled jigsaw puzzle where all pieces are there, but just don't seem to fit. Suggestion: preplan and rehearse in particular detail your opening and closing, along with transitions or bridges between your main points. Despite the importance of your facts and figures, most presentations lose and confuse their audiences because of speakers' difficulties in beginning, concluding, and linking. In all communication contexts, transitions are very important in maintaining an audience's interest.

3. *Dissipate unnecessary energy before the presentation.* Much nervousness manifests itself in fidgeting, pacing, inappropriate gestures, and rapid speech that rarely characterize your normal communication patterns. Some speakers find that if they build into their schedules some appropriate exercise before the presentation, their energies are freed toward appropriate enthusiasm, not unnatural and awkward-appearing nervous tension. For example, if Francine Fiscal is a distance runner, she may be tempted to forego her normal early morning run and use that time to cram a few extra facts into her presentation. However, her customary five miles may be more helpful to the presentation.

4. *Converse with the audience, rather than try to become an orator.* Try to speak with—rather than lecture at—listeners. A conversational style will not only be more palatable to business audiences, but it will help you mentally reframe the presentation from a *trial* or *test* (as many people are likely to see it) to a *talk*. This informalizes your task somewhat and encourages you to be extemporaneous.

5. *Avoid advertising what nervousness you do feel.* Francine might be tempted to say something like, "Wow, I have hardly ever done this, so bear with me. My knees are really shaking!" Although many listeners will certainly sympathize, such a comment does little to improve her credibility. Audiences may like some presenters enormously, but they usually make bottom-line business decisions on other grounds. They want to be confident about your recommendations, and your disclaimers undercut their confidence in you: disclaimers and apologies inhibit listeners from "claiming" the same conclusions you have advocated. A second problem with advertising your nervousness, of course, is that you risk focusing your own attention on it more than necessary.

6. *Involve your audience actively in the presentation.* When people vegetate as uninvolved listeners, attention naturally wanders

from content to such things as doodling, grocery lists, judging a speaker's wardrobe, nit-picking small points, and other peripheral matters. As you observe these distracted behaviors, you'll start to doubt yourself and worry about your effectiveness, thus becoming more nervous. Keeping your audience at least minimally involved is not a guaranteed antidote, but will usually help control your jitters. Consider these suggestions for low-level audience involvement:

- Maintain eye contact with as many audience members as is comfortable for you; they'll appreciate this demonstration of connection, and people who have your attention are more likely to give you theirs. This means engaging people individually rather than sweeping your eyes over the room.

- Use psychologically involving language, which requires listeners to dramatize choices, compare options, visualize situations, and place themselves in hypothetical contexts. For example, you might say, "Imagine yourselves in this same room in nine months, debating possible expansion. Will closing the Dayton plant now be a boon or a hindrance to those discussions? That's the kind of question we're facing here."

- Diversify your presentation with different styles and modes; for example, one person could begin the presentation with a few overheads demonstrating recent investment trends, then a speaker with a different verbal style might summarize findings and recommendations, with the first speaker finishing up, passing out notes on the presentation, and inviting audience questions addressed to either presenter.

7. *Immediately before rising to speak, focus on your breathing, not your text.* Most professional speakers successfully control excessive nervousness by small behavioral tricks or rituals just before rising to address an audience. One such helpful reminder comes from the *centering* discipline suggested by some Eastern philosophies. As you silently wait for your time to speak, make sure you are seated in a comfortable, straight, and stable posture. Then, also silently, draw in five to ten breaths, imagining with each one the route of the air as it descends to the center of your body at the diaphragm. Hold the breath for a second after each intake, then exhale gently. Your goal should be to accomplish these breaths in a calm, measured manner—and to think only of counting the breaths without considering anything else. Most people find that muscles relax, minds become more flexible and creative, and, perhaps most important, fears associated with the speaking experience begin to ebb.

Situation 1: Analyzing Communication Apprenhension

Recall the past three times you've spoken before an audience of four or more people. For each event:

1. Describe as many details about your own behaviors and others' reactions as you remember.

2. Describe all the symptoms of nervousness you can remember.

3. Analyze possible links between your nervousness levels and the unique circumstances in that situation. For example, were you more or less nervous when using visual aids? When speaking to a group of twenty rather than a group of four around a small conference table? When you had a large amount of information to summarize, or when you wanted to persuade the audience to take a certain action?

4. How might you have revised the presentations (or your preparation for them) using the suggestions of this section? Which approaches seem most applicable and valuable to you? Which seem less applicable and valuable?

Presentations Versus Speeches

Many executives mistakenly (and often selfishly) believe that because they are speaking, the audience is primarily interested in them. Perhaps in the best of all possible worlds where friendly people have unlimited time, no deadlines, and maximum interest in each other, they could share many of their personal feelings with their co-workers—and expect them to be fascinated. Unfortunately, the real world in which most of us work falls somewhat short of ideal; listeners at work, though they may like you very much, still must be primarily interested in the instrumental aspects (the outcomes) of your presentation.

In most professional speaking situations, you can probably assume these things about your audience: (1) they are busy; (2) on some level, they'd rather be somewhere else; (3) they want to spend their time efficiently; and (4) you—as a person—matter to them, but primarily in your capacity of helping them understand something they don't currently know. To help them, and therefore to help yourself, plan on giving business *presentations* rather than *speeches*.[4] According to one specialist in business communication, presentations are commitments by a speaker

---

[4] M. Holcombe and J. Stein, *Presentations for Decision Makers: Strategies for Structuring and Delivering Your Ideas* (Belmont, CA: Lifetime Learning Publications, 1983), 2.

or speakers to focus on a topic in order to help an audience do something; they are specific, and necessarily involve a direct evaluation by the audience of the worth of the speaker's commitment.[5] Presentations are pointed and lean. Speeches, on the other hand, are flabbier. In a speech, a person talks about himself or herself, about interesting topics in general, about wide-ranging implications of things. If presentations get slimmer as they go along, speeches get fatter. Francine Fiscal's team can't afford that.

Presentation Contexts: Individual and Group

Management consultant Thomas Leech observes that top management is using presentations as never before to review studies, requests, recommendations, and programs being undertaken by their employees.[6] Requests for new equipment, approval to pursue a new business line, review of planning for facility modernization, findings of a task report on employee morale—all will probably involve one or more presentations to higher and higher levels of management. The oral presentation may be the main avenue of communication, and key decisions may be based on the presentation. Such opportunities may involve either individual or team effort. Let's consider some of the basics of each type of approach.

Individual Presentations

Earlier chapters in this book have discussed the importance of developing a communication plan when making an oral presentation; you must analyze the context compared with your own purpose, analyze your audience, decide on the most crucial content for your presentation, create a tentative text, and then polish what you want to say relative to this audience's knowledge and need to hear it. Beyond these factors, however, you can enliven your presentations by following some more specific advice:

1. *Plan for spontaneity*. This suggestion may sound like a paradox, but it is one born out of the particular challenges of speaking to a live audience. The value of spontaneity is based on two interrelated observations of effective speakers. First, audiences appreciate extemporaneous speaking—that is, speaking that is both planned efficiently and spontaneous enough to take into

---

[5] R. Hoff, 3–7.

[6] T. Leech, *How to Prepare, Stage, and Deliver Winning Presentations* (New York, NY: American Management Association, 1982).

account the immediate circumstances of the presentation. Second, with experience comes the realization that not everything will run according to plans. Oral presentations, like live television, are particularly susceptible to Murphy's Law—things that *can* go wrong . . . *do* go wrong. Effective speakers, therefore, create contingency plans. For example, when your overhead projector malfunctions, do you know the data on the illustrated graph well enough to describe interrelationships vividly with a verbal explanation rather than relying on visual comparison? Part of planning for spontaneity, of course, involves setting up your room and equipment prior to the start of the presentation, and knowing where everything is located ("now, uh, . . . where's that light switch? Oh, uh, . . . could you get that for me?").

2. *Sensitize yourself to nonverbal cues.* The primary distinction between written and oral communication contexts is that speech situations allow a fuller range of human expression. Even though speech content is in many ways easier to plan for, the nonverbal aspects of your presentation will often make or break the occasion. Communication researchers, in fact, have estimated that 67 percent to over 90 percent of the meaning humans generate while communicating can come from the interpretation of nonverbal communication messages. A sensitivity to the nonverbal realm is even more critical because, according to psychologists, most people base their judgments about relationships primarily on nonverbal cues, and that when nonverbal and verbal behaviors of a speaker contradict each other (for example, a sweating and shaking speaker asserting "I'm confident you'll accept my suggestions"), the listener is likely to believe and put faith in the nonverbal message. Before and during your presentation, be aware of the following questions:

- Are you dressed appropriately for the occasion?

- Do you arrive on time? Do you keep an audience beyond the allotted or expected time?

- Are you speaking from a distance appropriate for your audience and room? Different distances are appropriate for different topics, interaction contexts, and persons. For example, in a large room, audiences will expect presenters to stand at the front at least ten or fifteen feet away, while many conference rooms seem to invite interaction distances of only four or five feet, and seated presentations.

- Does your voice indicate by its tone, rate, volume, and inflection that you are interested and credible in your topic area?

- Do you manipulate your materials and equipment confidently? For example, speakers who pass out complicated handouts that introduce ideas not yet covered in the presentation usually succeed only in distracting audiences. If handouts are necessary, match their complexity to the specific point for which they are used, and time their distribution appropriately. If you are using any type of projector, ensure your materials are in order, accessible, and the equipment is in good working order.

- Do you look listeners in the eyes? Few messages are more indicative of power relationships than eye contact patterns. Without staring, speakers are usually expected to connect visually with all audience members in small group gatherings. Of course, cross-cultural expectations are especially important in this regard, as they are with most nonverbal cues. Make certain you understand the eye contact patterns expected by the groups you are addressing.

- Are you appropriately animated in your gestures? Body movement can help your audience relate more directly to you and your commitment to the topic.

3. *Introduce the presentation by clarifying your own credibility*. Even if the time allotted to you is brief, don't launch directly into your recommendations and analysis without a short summary of who you are and what kind of work led you to this particular presentation. Without boasting, describe factually (a) your qualifications, if not known already by your audience; (b) the charge, or what you were asked to do; and (c) the extent of the research and preparation that led to the presentation.

For example, an accountant might say: "As some of you know, six months ago I was asked by our Administrative Vice President to investigate payroll procedures across all our subsidiaries. As you also might know, I worked on payroll matters when I was in public accounting. I spent about three months gathering data through collecting written reports and conducting face-to-face interviews, and another two months or so analyzing the procedures and investigating what similar firms are doing in streamlining payroll matters. My assistant, Fred Smith, and I wrote the report you received last week—and I'm here today to summarize the recommendations and answer any questions you may have."

4. *Preview the presentation for the audience, including how much time you believe it will take*. It's important for your audience to have a mental map of where you are going. Many speakers will forget

this step because they are nervous, launching directly into point one (or worse, point two or three). When this happens, audiences tend to get nervous. Especially in a business environment, people like to be assured that the person nominally in control of the time of a meeting (usually the speaker, in this case, you) understands the time constraints and has a realistic grasp of how information fits into those constraints. At this point, present your listeners with your *hook*, the basic reason that should motivate them to continue listening: "Adopting the plan I propose could save the firm several thousand dollars and hundreds of work hours per pay period."

5. *Stay with your planned organization unless audience reaction persuades you to deviate from it.* Although most content- and organization-related issues of oral presentations have been discussed in previous chapters, this point deserves special emphasis here. A truly extemporaneous style means that your presentation is connected both to the content plan you've already devised and to the audience whose reactions you can't fully predict. What should happen when, during a presentation, you sense (by comments or nonverbal reactions) that the audience already fully understands three of your four recommendations? Should discussion time *still* be evenly divided among the recommendations as planned? Although the answer seems obvious and logical, many inexperienced presenters unfortunately stick with their canned outline, no matter what. The audience suffers, as does the cause being advocated.

Remember, too, that if you've organized well, nearly everything you say should be relevant to some new action, changed behavior, or better policy that your audience can decide upon. Keep your emphasis on audience action; in other words, what should they do differently after hearing you? In this way, even an informational presentation (an informational briefing, for example, as background to a group's later discussion) has persuasive elements. At the very least, you are persuading them to take your information seriously.

6. *Review for impact.* Most presentations are short, so there is little time for elaborate closings. Still, you probably should practice a brief review that summarizes your main points and gives the listeners a strong reason for remembering what you've advocated. For example: "In the past fifteen minutes, you've heard three reasons why we might want to revise our payroll procedures. The first two reasons are direct bottom-line factors—streamlining office record-keeping will save money, and combining the responsibilities of several accountants will save both

money and time. The final reason is basic fairness—our employees will see us as more concerned with their welfare."

7. *Stress dialogue.* Many speakers mistakenly think presentations are one-way pipelines to an audience, similar to written communication. However, if this is the purpose, why arrange for the direct presence of an audience at all? People gather in groups to do more than just take in information; that can be done more efficiently through other communication modes. People come together, rather, to test ideas, to compare their judgments with others, to clarify ambiguities, and sometimes—frankly—to demonstrate directly that they know what they're talking about. Oral presentations, in other words, are social occasions. Don't treat them as mere one-way performances.

When concluding your presentation, be sure to ask for reactions, and don't be afraid of them when they come. Usually you will be the person in the room who knows the most about your specific topic, even if you won't necessarily be the one with the most power. In Chapter 6 we suggested that you deal with questions and replies through a simple three-stage approach: first, restate or clarify the question to the questioner's satisfaction, to prove that you understand; second, answer the question preferably by providing new information and by relating that information to earlier content from the talk; and third, check back with the questioner to verify that he or she at least feels understood (if not agreed with).

8. *Follow up the presentation with a realistic analysis of feedback.* In some situations (for example, in presenting workshops or training modules for employees) you will be expected to prepare and distribute evaluation forms for your audience to fill out and return, either to you or to a sponsoring agent. You can then assess whether and how your presentation met your goals. In less structured situations, your analysis will have to be based upon much more impressionistic information: how many listeners asked questions, who requested further information, the ultimate action the group took as a result of your information, the facial expressions of interest or disinterest, and so forth. Whether the feedback is precise or ambiguous, however, remember that the main goal of evaluation is to do better next time—not so you can relive all the pain and agony (or joy) of a past presentation. Feedback is not a time machine in which you travel backward through regrets, "should have dones," or celebrations; it is a forward-looking strategy for planning your next presentation and becoming a more successful professional.

CHAPTER EIGHT   161

Situation 2: Analyzing an Oral Presentation

Have a friend with a video camera tape your five-minute informal explanation of the major features of your favorite word processing or database program. Then,

1. Analyze the tape in terms of extemporaneous speaking criteria. That is, do you appear to be both prepared and informal?

2. Develop a plan to expand your five-minute explanation into a fifteen-minute presentation, complete with introduction, preview, visual aids, review, and question-and-answer period.

3. Ask your friend to tape your expanded presentation and then go over the two tapes with you. The two of you should focus on how well you maintained the extemporaneous style with the extra structure and responsibilities of the more formal presentation.

Group Presentations

Most of our reminders for individual presenters apply equally well to situations in which a team or group has prepared information for an audience. Obviously, some additional complications may arise in group presentations. For instance, team presentations may invite coordination problems and disorganization. Audiences can become confused by the intricate logistics of how group members juggle their materials, and even wonder "Who's in charge here?" Teams preparing presentations must constantly ask themselves whether the advantages of the team's presence and interaction at the presentation outweigh the potential liabilities.

Team presentations are especially appropriate when a small group of two to four professionals has worked equally on a project, or when each person in the team brings a special expertise to the situation. If a team presentation will best meet the needs of your task, you'll avoid some pitfalls if you remember to:

1. *Divide the labor carefully.* Ensure that your team's various tasks and how you divide them in the presentation make sense to listeners. For example, if there are four people in a presentation team, but one of them never speaks, the audience may wonder why he or she is there. Audiences find such things distracting. If all four members are to participate, provide four meaningful roles for them to perform. As appropriate, briefly clarify the various presentational roles for the audience and the different areas of expertise represented by the team members.

2. *Leave intragroup tensions at home.* Participating in a business presentation means that all team members are cooperatively giving the same pre-

sentation. Members of the team may have disagreed in the planning process about the content of recommendations or the ways they want to structure information. This is natural and normal. However, do not advertise such dirty laundry to an audience that doesn't need to hear about it. Loud sighs, dismissive glances, shaking the head to signal obvious disagreement, and verbal put-downs of other team members will weaken the impact of any presentation. The presentation is not normally the time or place to advertise disagreement, with the possible exception of when listeners sincerely inquire about possible disagreements. On certain extremely rare occasions, in groups with significant tension and content disagreement, a spokesperson might want to state calmly and simply that a particular issue "was difficult for us to decide, and not everyone in the group is fully convinced. However, we believe on balance that…". There is no need to identify who believes what.

3. *Designate a primary spokesperson.* He or she typically will handle introductions, transitions, summaries, and question-and-answer periods. A spokesperson need not be the formal leader of the group, or even the person with the highest status within the organization—although these are the most likely possibilities. The purpose of having a designated spokesperson, however, is pragmatic in that an audience needs to know whom to question for clarification and for insight.

We recommend that the spokesperson assume the role of coordinator rather than becoming the group's boss or authority figure. The differences may be subtle, but compare your own reactions to the two following statements: "I'd now like to call on Jim, who will provide you with what I think is our strongest recommendation"; and "Our next speaker is Jim, who did most of the work on the especially important Jackson Glove account." The first introduction spotlights the introducer as the leader, while the second clearly indicates the extent of Jim's contribution.

4. *Interrupt only to crisis-manage.* Few aspects of team presentations are more irritating to audiences than when presenters constantly talk over each other's words. Some interruptions are normal in any conversation, of course, and parts of most team presentations will become conversational. However, constant interruptions will give the impression that your group does not know what it is doing. That said, your group should still remember that some interruptions (for instance, for correcting misstatements of important statistics) are necessary. The spokesperson should usually be the one to interrupt in such cases.

5. *Practice transitions and team roles beforehand.* In many situations, we have observed groups of students and executives working well together in an extended project. Surprisingly, many of these groups assume that their work is finished when they've decided on content and have divided up the roles for their presentation. Members then each go their separate

ways until the appointed time when they reconvene, perhaps five minutes before the board meeting, to find that they haven't decided how to pass the conversational baton to each other within the presentation. The awkward and embarrassing moments this creates could be avoided by an hour or so of rehearsal the day before. At the rehearsal the group runs through its plan and makes final decisions about such matters as who goes first, how he or she will set the stage for the next speaker, how equipment needs are being handled, and how each person's responsibilities for content might affect what others will say.

6. *If possible, do a full rehearsal.* A full run-through allows a team to make needed adjustments. For example, one part of the presentation might be too long (or too short). Perhaps one presenter is using technical jargon the audience might not understand. While diverse styles are good, the whole presentation must hang together. You can also decide at this stage whether your audio-visual aids are appropriate and who will run equipment or change overhead transparencies during the presentation. Thus, at least one full dress rehearsal is useful.

Interviews to Gather Information

Your ability to make a persuasive and clear presentation to a group will depend upon a variety of factors. One obvious facet of success in an organization is the extent to which you are informed and prepared. Some information-gathering strategies depend upon your ability to do library research or extended personal research in databases or organizational files, such as we discussed in Chapter 4. Still other research strategies depend directly on your ability to relate to people in face-to-face communication situations. This is another crucial facet of the connection between accounting and communication.

Full preparation for your presentations will often involve interviews with key people both inside and outside your organization, eliciting the information that could become the very foundation for your best ideas. Effective interviewers understand that information can take many forms. Some interviews will be primarily for the purpose of determining the facts of a situation ("Who signs checks greater than $1,000?" or "In what form do you keep records from prior years?"); other interviews will ask for critical judgments of your respondents ("What did you think about Chrysler's decision to close the Austin plant rather than retool for the Caravan?"); while still others will probe the interviewee's feelings and personal preferences ("Would you be more comfortable with calling in outside consultants, or would you rather decide on the new software in-house?"). Interviews can also have political purposes. If you are going to make suggestions about someone else's turf, interviewing that person can provide information, generate critical support, identify problems, or be the professionally courteous thing to do.

Try to think of the term *interview* without a job interview's connotations of nervousness, and without the connotations of interrogation you'd associate with an IRS agent interviewing you about last year's taxes. Instead, consider the interview as literally an *inter-view*, an interpersonal conversation in which one person elicits information from another or others, yet each party gains some knowledge ("view") of the other through the relationship ("inter"). Although a fuller treatment of interviewing approaches is impossible here,[7] we will stress four major issues: preparation, questioning, listening, and recording.

Preparation

Unfortunately, an interview occasionally is conducted for purely selfish reasons. The interviewer could find out information on his or her own, but would rather short cut the process a bit by calling Carl or Carla and asking if they'd like to have lunch. During the hour of lunch, sometime near the second cup of coffee, comes: "Oh, by the way, could you fill me in on why the Mimico acquisition fell through? I've got a report to do for the home office. What was their financial baggage, anyway?" It's probably obvious the questioner doesn't have enough background in the situation, and is substituting this meeting for information-gathering that should be done by the researcher alone. The respondent, in effect, is offered a free lunch in order to help accomplish the questioner's work.

Many interviews, on the other hand, are absolutely necessary. Information you might discover in computer files, in company correspondence, and in the library will be incomplete without the context that key people in the organization can provide. Context is what surrounds an event, often determining how it should be interpreted. Context can include such factors as the history of a gradually emerging decision, the kind of time pressures in which a decision was made, or the interpersonal atmosphere of conflict from which an edict was issued. In addition to the obvious context factors, many organizational facts are not easily researched in the files simply because they aren't quantitative or even objective, but instead are contextual. They may be personal, value- or emotion-based, culture-specific within a given department or company, or oriented to future goals that may not yet be precisely articulated. All these factors define the human side of organizational life; they are the territory of the interview.

Be sure to do your homework before any interview. Not only should you familiarize yourself with relevant facts, but also make sure that

---

[7] See G. Killenberg and R. Anderson, *Before the Story: Interviewing and Communication Skills for Journalists* (New York, NY: St. Martin's Press, 1989).

you've read the key documents your respondent is likely to discuss, and that you are able to speak his or her language as much as possible. Some subgroups or jobs develop their own distinct **jargon**, their own specialized terminology for their distinct tasks and challenges. Some jargon terms may be linguistic shortcuts, in which a common or seemingly familiar word is used in a particularized meaning. Your company's legal department, for example, will prepare "briefs" that are anything but brief. Other jargon words may sound esoteric and unfamiliar if you don't work within a given group, but are used so frequently within that office that an interviewee usually won't think twice about using them in a conversation with you. In such circumstances, it is your responsibility to prepare yourself beforehand to converse as much as possible within the other person's field of information and language style. However, do not be afraid to ask for clarification.

Questions and the Interview Schedule

"What do I want to know?" is the question you, as the interviewer, have to answer. Adequate preparation gives you the answer to this basic orienting question of an interview and can lead to the specific questions you'll want to ask your respondent later. In essence, the answer to this orienting question signals the theme of your interview, just as each report you write should have a single point or theme that it develops. Although there will obviously be times when it's just not very clear what you want or need to know and the interview will have to be somewhat exploratory, in most business settings interviews are expected to have a clear focus. The interviewer, even if she or he is of a lesser status in the organization, is expected to propel the interview forward with appropriate and well-chosen questions that are built upon what the respondent actually says.

This advice seems to contradict what novice interviewers believe an interview should be. They naively think that an interview is a tidy sequence of questions that primarily build on each other, that lead to a rational point or the possibility of a logical conclusion. This is a misconception that derails more interviews than it assists. In contrast, the interviewer's essential task, in effect, is assisted talk—he or she wants to help the other person elaborate on information, explain motivations, and provide context. This rarely happens as a result of predecided questions, but often develops within an interchange that has a conversational quality to it. The questions don't necessarily build on each other, but build on the responses.

What does this mean for the interviewer preparing to meet an interviewee? Simply put, our advice is to prepare a **tentative interview schedule** based on what you need to know as a result of the meeting. The schedule is a short and coherent list of questions (often 5 to 8 in brief interviews) on issues you assume are important. The order of questioning may be chronological, cause-effect, problem-solution, or some other pattern of your choice. The main value of this schedule is to act as the spine of the interview, its central support if things seem to be tottering. However, don't assume that the asking and answering of such questions is the interview itself. Be flexible and prepared to redirect the interview toward side trips of meaning that may be suggested within the conversation. If you are overly committed to just going down a list of questions, you might miss important information. Be careful to listen and reflect before going on. In addition, avoid framing your next question while the person you're interviewing is still responding to your current question.

Based on how well you listen to your respondent, you should be reminded of secondary questions designed to follow up or clarify his or her statements; these follow-ups, usually called **probe questions** by experienced interviewers, may not even be questions in the normal sense. For example, you might probe with comments such as: "You're concerned about the reorganization," or "I'm noticing that when you talked about the Pepsi contract you mentioned several projections, but just now, on the Dr. Pepper deal, the matter seems less defined." A question may be implied by the probe, but it's one that the respondent may choose to answer in a variety of ways. Other examples of probing styles:

"Seems to me you think the company's 1992 responses were stronger than those of recent years."

"That's an interesting point. Could you say more about the tax implications of that?"

"I'm not sure I understand why the report was released to the press."

Questions are indispensable in interviewing, but they can have implications for relationships. First, asking a question might suggest that the interviewer is deficient, ignorant in a given area and in need of the help of a more experienced, *higher status* person. This is especially true if a question is asked in a tone of subservience, or asked in a reticent, retiring, or tentative way. Most psychological states (e.g., scared, subservient, pleading) are signaled by messages of voice (e.g., pitch, volume), posture, gesture, and eye contact. A too-soft, quavering voice coming from an interviewer with averted eyes is unlikely to impress corporate interviewees. Therefore, be aware that how you ask certain questions, and even the act of questioning itself, can undercut your status and position within an organization. It is one thing to be appropriately respectful of a superior, for instance, but quite another thing to advertise an inappropriately deferential self-concept. Consider your questioning style carefully, and ask questions assertively.

Second, questioning someone could unfortunately suggest the opposite power message—it can take on an interrogative tone, implying that the person queried is of *lower status* and on the spot. Often, as in a courtroom or a classroom, people don't ask questions because they need or want answers but because they are trying to test another person's ability to answer. In daily life, people often use questions sarcastically to substitute for negative statements they're reluctant to make openly. This is why being questioned often stimulates defensiveness. Even such seemingly innocent questions as, "Why did you do that?" might be interpreted by another person as really meaning, "You should have done something else," "That was stupid," or "You should have asked someone else about it before you decided things on your own." Again, most of this kind of meaning is implied by your nonverbal demeanor and vocal tone. In the successful interview, you neither undercut your own status (whatever it may be) nor undercut the position of the other; you talk with the other person about issues of mutual concern.

Listening

Your interviewing skill will to some extent depend on your listening skill. Unfortunately, most executives assume that while they may need training in public speaking, listening is somehow a more natural and automatic human activity, much like breathing. Yet, it too should receive increased attention and skill practice, since it's the other half of improved oral communication. We make some basic suggestions for improving listening behavior that should help your interviews progress more smoothly. You may want to consult other specialized sources for more information on this vital communication skill.[8]

By listening carefully, you'll learn more than by just robotically recording replies to the canned questions you'd planned before ever walking into the room or placing the call. Although most people assume listening is a process of simply taking in or receiving oral messages, it is considerably more complicated than that. Listeners not only *hear* messages (respond at the physiological level to sound waves) but inevitably *interpret* them as well. The process of listening involves integrating new oral messages into the meaning patterns already established in the listener, and the subsequent modification of those patterns.

What can this definition mean at a practical level for you as an interviewer? Simply, it suggests a series of reminders:

1. *When listening, you will be prejudiced.* You must learn to recognize and take into account your own biases, since psychologists tell us that it's impossible for you to check them at the door. The decision to listen to someone means that your biases are already at work, perhaps distorting what they say to fit better into what

---

[8] See D. Borisoff and M. Purdy (Eds.), *Listening in Everyday Life: A Personal and Professional Approach* (Lanham, MD: University Press of America, 1991).

you already believe or expected to hear in the first place. Alternatively, your listener's bias may at times exaggerate the contrast between your perception of the speaker's meaning and what you believe. In any case, no listener can receive messages in a totally objective, unprejudiced way; new messages are inevitably related to old patterns (biases). Don't assume that your interpretation is what the other person means. It would be safer to assume that what he or she means is never precisely what you've interpreted.

2. *Your listening style will be observed and evaluated by speakers.* Don't assume that just because listening is an inner cognitive process, your listening style won't be obvious to your interviewee. People tend to signal their listening to companions by displaying certain behaviors. In Western culture, for example, listeners tend (with certain exceptions) to maintain consistent, but not constant eye contact with speakers; to orient their posture generally toward speakers; to nod, say "uh-huh" occasionally, or otherwise confirm that speakers have indeed been heard; to avoid both subsidiary tasks (reading a newspaper while listening) and nonverbal barriers (such as dark glasses); and to participate periodically by contributing to the flow of conversation. In the absence of such behavior, speakers tend to assume that they're not being listened to. Thus, your listening style will often directly determine the amount and kind of information others are willing to share. If they feel as though you're a poor listener, don't care, or wouldn't understand, then obviously they'll curtail their talk with you.

3. *When listening effectively, you'll identify and empathize with speakers.* If listening naturally involves your own biases, then effective listening designed to gain insight must somehow invite meanings that go beyond your prior experience. This happens through **empathy**—the willingness to imagine another person's experience from his or her perspective, remembering all the while that you can't give up your own perspective. Although some training programs teach empathy as a behavioral technique, we prefer to think of it as an *attitude of communication* by which you remind yourself that your interviewee's perspective is both important and separate from your own. Empathizing is different from sympathizing: sympathy is associated with feelings for the other person (often in a sad or negative situation), whereas empathy is a more generalized willingness to try to experience things as the other person does in his or her situation, as he or she experiences it. Remember that you don't have to agree with, or even like, a person in order to empathize.

4. *When listening effectively, you'll check often on the other person's meanings.* This approach, often called active listening, is essential if you want to convince others that you care about what they say. Listening actively should reflect your genuine interest in people and what they have to say. If you are in fact understanding the other person's message, occasionally demonstrate this by paraphrasing their ideas. You are not trying merely to repeat their words back to them as a parrot or a tape recorder would, but instead are demonstrating how you are interpreting their ideas. At times, you might even want to go beyond what they've said overtly to check out a new impression you've started to develop without much evidence. As examples, active listeners might use such comments and internal summaries as:

"Your main point seems to be . . ."

"I think what you're getting at is . . ."

"I think you're saying that you've got two responses to the merger—that you're ambivalent, and that . . . "

"Somehow, today you seem more pleased by this directive than when we talked last month. Am I wrong?"

Remembering and Recording

No matter how well you listen in an interview, you will not remember everything. The decisions you make about how to record and recall information will directly affect the value of the interviewing. Actually, these decisions also significantly affect how the interviewee will interact with you during the conversation. Let's survey several of your options for retaining interview information.

First, the most traditional and time-tested method of recording an interview is to take extensive notes. The advantage of **notetaking** is that it is relatively unobtrusive and combines a reasonable ability to be thorough with the possibility of devising your own system of abbreviation or shorthand. Unfortunately, the more extensive your notetaking becomes, the less you can maintain visual contact with and nonverbal sensitivity to your conversation partner. If you choose to take notes, we suggest that you (1) be as unobtrusive as possible in your writing (shuffling stacks of papers will usually distract both parties); (2) take notes only (but always) when the respondent discusses an important and germane point; and (3) key your notes to the interview schedule you've tentatively planned beforehand. The planned interview topics or questions might be jotted down on the left-hand side of a page (or each at the top of a series of pages in a small notebook) with plenty of space to the right of each topic for noting the other's responses.

A second approach preferred by many experienced interviewers could be called **delayed notetaking**; in this method, you postpone written reactions until immediately after the interview. The key to delayed notetaking is to conduct the interview with maximum alertness and then set aside about thirty minutes after the interview itself to reconstruct on paper the key information from the interview. At this time, review the schedule of questions and topics, jotting down what significant replies the respondent made. Also, don't forget to note the tone of the other's talk, if relevant, and any specific documents or sources he or she gave you during the interview. Sometimes you find that documents have been misplaced; mention of them in your notes can help solve this potential mystery.

One important suggestion: even if you plan to use a delayed approach to notetaking, you should carry a notepad into an interview, if only to be prepared for a situation where the respondent asks or expects you to remember something specifically. Your notepad, even if you use it sparingly, can be reassuring to your interviewee in a professional context. Of course, there is no reason why you couldn't combine judicious notetaking within the interview with a private review session afterward; this combined strategy can only increase your thoroughness.

A third option should be reserved for the times when exactness of detail is your foremost criterion. Consider the possibility of **tape recording** an interview—preferably with a microcassette recorder or other small unobtrusive cassette recorder placed slightly to the side of the conversation. Ask your respondent first if he or she is comfortable with the recorder, and then, even with agreement, be sensitive to signals (fidgeting, constant glances toward the machine, comments about the taping process) that might indicate discomfort. If you have doubts about the appropriateness of taping, don't use it. The extra information that some public sphere interviewers such as reporters get from taping an interview is usually not worth the tradeoff you'll make in an informal organizational context. For example, a reporter may need to enliven a story with quotations, but for most organizational research purposes, context and basic factual information will be much more crucial than a respondent's exact wording.

In sum, the process of interviewing can be seen as the skill of focused conversation. It is a conversation in which one person approaches the interaction with a need for information or insight that another presumably possesses, and a conversation in which the interviewer facilitates the interviewee's sharing of that information. It is not a mechanical process, but rather a potentially enjoyable way for people to learn about the organization. Still, however enjoyable the process is for participants, practical interviewing must be efficient, effective, and informative.

Situation 3: Practicing an Interview

Videotape or audiotape an interview of an economist or other financial expert from a program such as PBS's "Wall Street Week."

1. Identify in the tape any potential misunderstandings by the interviewer, or points where viewers could easily misinterpret or be confused about what the expert is saying.

2. For each potential incident of "missed meaning," write out a probe response that would paraphrase the expert in order to check on, clarify, or specify your perception of his or her intended meaning. Remember in doing this that you are not mind reading the intentions of the expert; a "perception check" or "active listening response" like this can be just as productive if you turn out to be wrong in your paraphrase—the result is increased understanding.

Summary

Accountants, like Francine Fiscal, often find themselves in a variety of oral communication contexts, and need to anticipate how these situations can affect their credibility within an organization. Perhaps you hope you will be evaluated exclusively on the basis of your professional accounting expertise—your facility with computers, with analyzing complex trends, with projecting figures into the next decade. Rightly or wrongly, however, others tend to form and maintain their impressions of you based largely on how you conduct yourself in presentations and interpersonal relationships.

This chapter has not surveyed every possible oral communication context in which you'll find yourself. Instead, we've concentrated on helping you overcome the basic problem (for many) of communication apprehension, to improve your presentational speaking style, and to interview others meaningfully. Mastering these skills can increase your self-confidence and boost your career potential.

How to Approach a Selected Situation

Situation 1: Analyzing Communication Apprenhension

1. This activity depends to a great extent on your attention to concrete detail. Without prejudging the importance of the specific facts of your speaking situations, list as many details as possible. The kinds of detail many people recall might include:

   About themselves:

   What was I wearing?

   What kind of notes did I use?

   Did my talk include visual aids?

   How long did I talk?

   Did I maintain eye contact with the majority of audience members?

   Did I stand or sit while presenting?

   About audience and situation:

   How were the audience members dressed?

   What time of day was my presentation?

   How many people attended?

   What shape was the table (or other seating arrangement) in the room?

   Did people ask questions?

   Was I expected to speak for a long time?

2. Symptoms of nervousness that some people experience include:

   Excessive perspiration

   Dry mouth

   Shaking of arms and legs

   Forgetting important points or jumbling organization

   Quavering voice

   Inability to look directly at audience members

   Increased rate of speech

   Flushed, red face and neck

   Noticeably increased awareness of heartbeats

3. Develop some tentative hypotheses about how you, your situation, and your speech anxieties are related. This exercise will not prove exactly what causes your nervousness, but if you can identify some tentative linkages between certain tasks, situations, and audiences on one hand, and your level of nervousness on the other, then you'll be better able to diagnose and avoid some unnecessary triggers for nervousness. To expand on one possible scenario: Suppose you determine that in several speaking situations your symptoms of nervousness or stage fright are especially noticeable when you're asked to explain numerous specific details, but in other situations—explaining a recommendation, for instance—you're relatively calm. What does this tell you?

4. If one of your nervousness triggers seems to be the task of describing precise details, you might remind yourself to supplement your preparation with transparencies, computer-generated graphics, or bullet-point handouts that carry much of the weight of the content for you. As you do so, remember that some handout and visual aid strategies can detract from the impact of presentations. Use the visuals as cues for your explanations, as checklists, and as indicators of the complexity of your topic, but not as direct substitutes for your own analysis. Rehearse your talk thoroughly by practicing how and when you will refer conversationally to the visual supplements.